GRIDLOCK

Gridlock

Crossword Puzzles and the Mad
Geniuses Who Create Them

Matt Gaffney

Thunder's Mouth Press
New York

GRIDLOCK: *Crossword Puzzles and the Mad Geniuses Who Create Them*

Published by
Thunder's Mouth Press
An imprint of Avalon Publishing Group, Inc.
245 West 17th Street, 11th floor
New York, New York 10011

AVALON
publishing group incorporated

Library of Congress Cataloging-in-Publication Data is available.

ISBN-10: 1-56025-890-X
ISBN-13: 978-1-56025-890-2

9 8 7 6 5 4 3 2 1

Book design by Maria E. Torres

Printed in the United States of America
Distributed by Publishers Group West

Dedicated to:

Henry Hook
Merl Reagle
Mike Shenk
Jordan Lasher (1946–1995)
Jack Luzzatto (1909–1991)
A.J. Santora (1919–2005)

a young man's inspirations

Contents

Introduction and Acknowledgments

The world outlined in this book—people who write and edit crossword puzzles—is a small one, just a few hundred people in size. Everyone pretty much knows everyone else; there are some rivalries, but actual strife is rare. Many of the people mentioned herein are professional colleagues of mine, and I have direct business dealings with several of them, usually mentioned where relevant in the text. The majority of my crossword work these days, however, falls outside the realm of professional puzzle writers and editors.

As Will Rogers did, I like almost everyone I meet, in both crosswords and in general life, and have no axes to grind with anyone mentioned in this book. The opinions I express here are as genuine and uninfluenced by financial considerations and personal relationships as I can make them.

I'd like to thank and acknowledge the following people:

For their assistance in various aspects of writing this book: Eric Albert, Chris Begley, Eric Berlin, Jon Delfin, Tyler Hinman, Henry Hook, Mark Hsu, Frank Longo, Stan Newman, Rich Norris, Trip Payne, Ellen Ripstein, and Byron Walden.

For getting me hooked on puzzles as a kid, my sister Rebecca Gaffney.

For editing the manuscript with élan, John Oakes and Lukas Volger at Thunder's Mouth Press.

For selling the book, my literary agent Janet Rosen at Sheree Bykofsky Associates, and Sheree herself.

For answering many questions with patience and clarity, two special notes of thanks to Will Shortz and Peter Gordon.

CHAPTER 1

Stamford

Sudoku 1, crosswords 0. Not good.

Sudoku 2, crosswords 0. Sheesh.

Sudoku 3, crosswords 0. Painful.

Two bubbly, chattering teenaged girls sitting side by side, solving sudoku together from an oversized book. Sudoku 5, crosswords 0. This is really discouraging.

I'm riding an Amtrak train headed to Stamford, Connecticut, for the 29th annual American Crossword Puzzle Tournament, the largest such contest in the country, and making my way to the café car. As I negotiate the swaying aisles, I'm counting the number of passengers solving sudoku and the number solving crosswords. As a professional cruciverbalist, I'm depressed by the results: my beloved crossword puzzles are getting totally shut out so far. The two teenaged girls I found especially galling—even the cool kids in high school are solving sudoku now. I certainly don't remember them solving crosswords when I was in high school.

A few rows later, I pass an enormously obese man solving sudoku from a newspaper and am ashamed to find the words "you fat bastard" passing through my brain. Sudoku 6, crosswords 0.

Finally, that rarest of birds emerges into view: there on my right, a blond-haired guy with glasses is solving a *crossword puzzle*. Yes! From *GAMES Magazine* no less, which means it must be a highbrow puzzle. For a moment my faith in the common man is restored: this sudoku thing is just a fad, and the good ol' American crossword puzzle we all know and love will reassert its dominance in the nation's cultural heart any day now. Take that, high school girls!

But then my heart sinks, as I realize that this isn't the "common man" at all—it's Dave Tuller, a well-known crossword constructor who's finished in the top 15 at the tournament each of the past three years he's competed, including two 4th place results. Sigh. The only people solving crosswords over sudoku on this train are the die-hards, practicing en route to this weekend's battleground.

I know Dave—he's the only other well-known crossword constructor besides me who lives in the DC area—so I say hi and suggest we ride up together. I move my stuff and we begin catching up—he's buying a house, hasn't solved many puzzles in the past year, is hoping to return to top 10 placement in the tournament after what he labels his "disappointing" 13th-place finish (out of 467 entrants) the previous year. Busy with a new job, he says, "I hadn't solved a single crossword all year before last year's tournament."

"Is that literally true?" I ask. "Not a single one?"

"Well, I solved a few variety puzzles, but I can't remember an actual crossword. I can't guarantee that the number is zero—it may be modulo one or two."

Tuller has a Ph.D. in mathematics from the University of Colorado, and I vow to look up later what "modulo" means. He's just turned thirty and looks like tennis champ Boris Becker, and carries the slightly haughty demeanor of an ultra-bright math junkie who generally assumes his audience knows words like "modulo," even if they don't. Most people at the crossword tournament probably will, though; somewhat counterintuitively, math-based professionals are well-represented among top crossword constructors and solvers.

Our train hits a typical Amtrak delay in Philadelphia. "This train's engine has experienced a malfunction and needs to be fixed," the conductor squawks through an ear-piercing announcement on P.A. equipment that looks Soviet-manufactured. "We're expecting a fifteen to twenty minute delay." In fact, the train won't leave for another hour.

"Play some hangman?" I ask Tuller.

"Sure," he agrees.

I get out a pad and pen. We decide on the sixth miss being gallows time and using only six-, seven-, or eight-letter words, since allowing shorter ones makes the game too hard, a simple word like FOX being borderline unguessable with five wrong letters or fewer.

I choose first, and mark six blank spaces, having chosen in my mind the word ZEPHYR (definition: a gentle breeze).

"A," Tuller guesses, earning himself a head.

"N" he says, and I gleefully draw a torso.

He hits with his next two guesses, R and E, but even so, I'm feeling good. He's probably going to burn a couple of body parts on vowels with his next two, and probably get hung soon thereafter, since Z, P, H, and Y are all high-scoring

Scrabble letters he's unlikely to toss out there. I'm mentally congratulating myself on word choice when Tuller shrugs and announces:

"Z."

Unreal. "You know it?" I ask.

"ZEPHYR," he condescends, like I even needed to ask. "Pretty typical hangman word. My turn."

As we rot in Philadelphia's 30th Street Station, the passengers around us yammer and eat and flip open laptops and somewhere, I suppose, Amtrak engineers are busy fixing that pesky engine. I don't notice the activity, though—I'm 100 percent focused on puzzling out Tuller's word, which he's marked out at six spaces, since I'm irked not only that he got ZEPHYR, but that he insinuated it was a hackneyed choice on my part.

"E," I guess. Head.

"A." Torso.

"U." Left leg.

"I." Right leg.

"O." Left arm. Only one guess left, but now I've got him: the word has to be RHYTHM, since no other six-letter word I can think of contains none of the five main vowels.

"RHYTHM," I announce.

"Nope," Tuller grins. Right arm. I'm dead.

I give the blank spaces another look and groan, realizing my error. "Shit, it's SYZYGY, right?"

Tuller nods. "I figured if you were going to do ZEPHYR, I had to do SYZYGY."

Syzygy. Definition: two opposing points in the moon's orbit.

Now I'm feeling extra-stupid, since he not only guessed my overused hangman word, but stumped me with his. And then I'm feeling extra-extra stupid, since Tuller follows up by asking, "Why didn't you just guess the Y instead of guessing RHYTHM? Then you'd've gotten SYZYGY easy."

This is really demoralizing. "Yeah, I just didn't think there could've been any other 6-letter words besides RHYTHM that didn't have A, E, I, O, or U."

Tuller thinks for a second, staring straight ahead at the back of the seat in front of him.

"Actually, it could've been CRWTHS," he says. "A CRWTH is some kind of Welsh musical instrument."

Later, at the tournament, I'll be telling this story to a half dozen people, and after I explain that I had guessed RHYTHM because I'd forgotten about SYZYGY and couldn't think of any other words that fit the pattern, two of the half dozen will simultaneously call out "CRWTHS!" This is the level of wordplay psycho the American Crossword Puzzle Tournament attracts.

Somewhere in northern New Jersey, Tuller and I head to the café car. I count three people working on sudoku, including one solving on his laptop, and zero solving crosswords. That's 9-1 in favor of sudoku, Tuller being the 1. As we wait in line, I mention my puzzle-counting game to him, and he looks perplexed.

"That wasn't a crossword I was solving," he says. "That was a crossword variant of some kind." Apparently, it had only looked like a crossword in the brief glance I'd gotten at it.

Sudoku 9, crosswords 0. Terrible.

The American Crossword Puzzle Tournament (ACPT) is held every spring at the Stamford Marriott, a building with Mecca status for crossword folk. With an eye toward filling their hotel for a weekend, the Marriott approached then-*New York Times* crossword editor Eugene T. Maleska about a tournament in the late 1970s. Maleska declined, but passed the idea on to up-and-coming puzzler Will Shortz, then all of twenty-five years old, and Shortz ran with it, attracting 149 participants to the inaugural tournament in 1978. When Maleska died in 1993, the *Times* hired Shortz to replace him as their crossword editor; twenty-eight years after he first christened it, Shortz is still directing the ever-growing tournament, which hit 500 entrants (on the dot) in 2006.

Friday night, the hotel lobby overflows with hugs, crossword shirts, luggage, handshakes, shrieks of recognition, and digital camera flashes. Greetings chirp high into the lobby's atrium as groups of puzzlers who haven't seen each other in a year get reacquainted. Circulating among the ever-shifting clusters I find 2001 champion Ellen Ripstein and 1984 champion John McNeill discussing their chances for the weekend. Both are past fifty in age, and the rising younger generation is very much on their minds—the 2005 tournament was won by twenty-year-old Tyler Hinman, after all.

"This is my first year wearing glasses at the tournament," Ripstein kvetches. "They have those large print clues, but I can't even see the numbers on those!"

"Oh,YEAH!" laughs McNeill, a jolly Texan, pointing to his own glasses.

"Your problem is"—here Ripstein points at McNeill "that you're still fast, but you sometimes make mistakes, and you just can't make mistakes anymore. These young kids now, they don't even read all the clues, they just go, 'oh, that looks like a word,' and move on."

Moving on, I spot *New York Sun* crossword editor Peter Gordon; Amy Reynaldo, a top solver whose blog "Diary of a Crossword Fiend" features her solving times for up to six newspapers' puzzles every day; and Jim Jenista, a constructor dressed, typically for him, in a tattered "crossword tuxedo," which consists of a bunch of paper crossword grids he's stitched imperfectly together. It is an understatement to say that the tuxedo fails to cover his entire body, and for reasons not entirely clear, he is also wearing a bike helmet plastered with crossword grids.

The tournament itself consists of seven puzzles that all 500 entrants will solve (or attempt to, anyway). Judges, of which I am one, will score them based on accuracy and speed, and the top three finishers will battle it out for the title on Sunday on a final championship puzzle, which they'll solve on oversized grids with dry erase markers before a packed-house audience. The winner will take home $4,000 and a boatload of geek street cred, the latter of which is probably the greater incentive.

But that all starts tomorrow: Friday night is just for fun, and the evening activity is a team trivia contest written and moderated by *Jeopardy!* uber-champ Ken Jennings. It's a huge coup that Shortz has recruited Jennings, the boyish Utah computer programmer who became a cult celebrity by winning seventy-four shows in a row, to emcee tonight's event.

As the crowd files into the ballroom for the trivia contest,

I spot Jennings standing alone behind the judge's table and introduce myself.

"I know exactly who you are," he replies with a Mormon nod. "I'm a big fan of your puzzles." My ego goes through the roof, and we discuss a mutual friend for a couple of minutes. Then someone taps me on the shoulder and I turn away, just as Byron Walden, a top crossword writer from California, moves over to introduce himself to Jennings.

"Yes, hello," I overhear Jennings tell him. "I'm a big fan of your puzzles."

Testing a theory, a few minutes later I eavesdrop as crossword legend Merl Reagle makes his way over to Jennings and introduces himself. I come to rue my nosiness when Jennings tells Reagle that he's a big fan of his puzzles, with an emphasis on the "big" that was lacking we when we'd spoken. I'm sure Jennings is sincere in knowing our names and puzzles, but I vow I'll never eavesdrop again (at the closing awards banquet on Sunday, North Carolina puzzle writer Harvey Estes tells me, unprompted, "You know, I was flattered when Ken Jennings said he knew my name and my puzzles, but then I realized—hey, that's not really such a big deal, since Ken Jennings knows *everything*.").

Trivia Time: per Jennings' instructions, the crowd of 450 breaks themselves into teams of four; judges then pass out papers with KenJen's forty questions on them, and teams have twenty minutes to write down their answers. They confer in hushed tones on questions that range from total gimmes ("What's the only Ivy League University in Rhode Island?") to medium-level pop culture references ("What breakfast cereal mascot is less known by his given names

'Horatio Magellan'?") to real head-scratchers ("How many rays are there on the Statue of Liberty's Crown?"). Answers: Brown, Cap'n Crunch, seven.

The top two teams, each of whom answered thirty-eight of the forty questions right, then take the stage for a College Bowl–style smackdown moderated by Jennings, who speaks so quickly that I can't understand several of the questions. The audience, which probably numbers modulo zero non-*Jeopardy!* fans, is thrilled with Jennings' appearance, and they line up to talk with him after the contest.

The schmoozing carries on at the wine and cheese reception; later, groups of two or eleven or five stake out far-flung corners of the main ballroom. They'll stay up way too late jousting over wordplay, home-written *Jeopardy!* rounds, and obscure board games. For a while I play "Initials" with a mixed-sex clique of twentysomethings; I only place fourth, but I'm happy with some of my two-pointers—meaning people no one else wrote down—like country singer Dwight Yoakam for D.Y. and author Sherwood Anderson for S.A. A pretty blonde gets three points, and many props from the gang, for being the only player to come up with an acceptably famous Y.O.*

2 AM Wooden game pieces click against cardboard surfaces, and the occasional peal of laughter springs from a far-off band of eight people playing a card-based game I've never seen before. I'm having a useful blast discussing angles on the crossword book market with a small group of middle-aged editors, but there's a tournament to officiate in the morning, so it's off to bed. The others agree, but just

*Yoko Ono.

outside the ballroom we run into another editor we know, and jaw about books for another half hour. I could do this all night, but I shouldn't, so I don't.

Saturday morning, Round 1: Tournament Director Will Shortz takes the mike and welcomes the packed ballroom to the 29th annual ACPT. With a comedian's timing and delivery, Shortz warms the crowd up—and calms their nerves—with his traditional reading of the most humorous letters he's received from solvers in the past year: "Dear Mr. Shortz: In the Jan. 11 crossword, 13-down seeks a five-letter answer for the clue 'Ragu rival.' The answer is PREGO. In truth, Prego is so far superior to Ragu that to call them rivals is to elevate one and belittle the other to such an extent that I am forced to conclude you have never tried Prego's Four-Cheese or Chunky Vegetable varieties . . ."

Now that they're loosened up, Shortz goes over the tournament rules: no talking; no reference tools of any kind allowed; turn off all cell phones before each round. The huge digital clock at the ballroom's edge is set at 15:00, and Shortz announces: "On your marks, get set, begin!" 500 hands turn 500 sheets of white paper over simultaneously; it looks and sounds like a low wave crashing onto a beach.

Besides reading the best-of solver letters, Shortz has another way to calm tournament rookies at the start of the competition: the first round's puzzle is always an easy one. This year it's written by Harvey Estes and titled "Step On It." The theme entries are all clued with those three words, and they're all things you step on: WELCOME MAT, DOCTOR'S SCALE, and so forth.

The judges stake out areas of the room and scan the horizon for raised hands, the official signal that a contestant has completed their puzzle. When a hand goes up, the nearest judge scurries over, takes the contestant's paper, and writes on it the number of minutes remaining on the big digital clock. The completed puzzles are rushed upstairs to the Judges' Room, where they're scored for accuracy and speed, and the contestant's total for that puzzle is entered into a computer.

I'm not surprised when the first hand to go up in Round 1 is that of wunderkind Tyler Hinman, the college senior who won the tournament last year at age twenty. The clock reads 12:05, which means it took Hinman less than three minutes to finish the crossword. In more difficult rounds to come, collecting papers is not particularly stressful; but in this first round, the puzzle is such a softball that judging feels like playing Whack-a-Mole. By the time you've collected one paper, two more hands have shot up in your vicinity, and you've got to instantly prioritize which one it makes sense to go after first.

Communicating with other judges is key—a helpful assist to a temporarily overtaxed colleague will leave your territory unpatrolled, but you've got to have faith that another judge will pick up your slack. At one point in Round 1, veteran judge Nancy Parsons and I wordlessly engineer a complete switch of the two sections we've been covering, like basketball defensemen who suddenly switch players off a pick.

The Judges' Room is a small, nondescript warren tucked away on the hotel's second floor behind a small maze of mirrors, hallways, and doors. Although it's my second year officiating, I still get lost half the time I try to find it over the weekend. Like the Smurfs' village, its location seems to magically change.

Just five small tables fit inside, but it's in this tiny space that tournament fates are decided. Judges slash orange, blue, and lime green pens across incorrect letters and words, then hand the stacks over to have the final scores keyed into the computer.

Harvey's Round 1 puzzle is easy, and almost everybody gets it right. The first mistake I come across is at 45-down, where someone has written in the incorrect TRAUMA instead of the correct TRANCE for the clue "Stupefied state." Not a bad guess, but the solver clearly didn't look at the crossing words on this one. It's a typical rookie mistake: Shortz is constantly advising solvers to take an extra minute when they're done with the puzzle to check their work over for errors, since the extra minute costs only twenty-five points, while turning in a perfectly-solved puzzle earns a 150-point bonus. It's worth it, but many solvers still rush, especially newbies.

As I'm marking papers, I hear judge Mike Shenk scrutinizing a puzzle over at another table. "It could be an O that they just didn't write very well," Shenk says, holding the paper right up close to his face. He grimaces, then hands it back to the judge who was asking his opinion. "I'd say we give them the benefit of the doubt on that."

Indeed, much of the banter in the Judges' Room revolves around handwriting and its decipherment. With 500 time-pressed people squeezing letters into small boxes—letters all 500 seem to write in completely different ways—penmanship quickly becomes a hot topic.

If a letter's identity is not clear, the first step is to compare it to other letters the solver wrote, since handwriting varies wildly. One solver writes the Greek letter lambda instead of a regular L; as long as she writes all her L's that way, that's fine. A paper I'll have later in the tournament features about half the E's in the grid written in uppercase letters and half of them written lowercase; bizarre, but not punishable.

Judge Joe DiPietro is amazed in Round 1 when he finds a contestant has taken the time to use Wite-Out on his puzzle: "Can't you see this guy just sitting there while the clock's running, waiting for it to dry?"

In close calls, as Shenk noted, judges generally try to give the letter to the contestant. If intent can be reasonably inferred, the solver gets the letter; for instance, even if a solver writes in a correct letter, then erases it, then doesn't put anything else in the square, tournament rules dictate that the square is counted as correct.

We didn't know it at the time, but handwriting would later light up Sunday morning's final round with a controversy that affected the very top of the leaderboard. "It wouldn't be Stamford if there wasn't a scoring controversy," a judge will later lament. With 500 contestants scratching in answers to 3,500 puzzles, you'd better believe that scoring is an inexact science.

Round 2 is a tougher puzzle, and in the Judges' Room we start to see the first recurring mistake of the tournament. At 29-across, a six-letter entry clued as "*In the Bedroom* co-star, 2001," tons of solvers are putting the incorrect Kevin SPACEY instead of the correct Sissy SPACEK.

It's a trappy clue and entry for a tournament puzzle—*In the Bedroom* was a fairly but not extremely well-known movie, and time-pressed solvers with a six-letter star of a 2001 film starting with S-P-A-C-E aren't likely to prioritize checking the down word that crosses it. How many movie stars' surnames could possibly fit that pattern, after all? Two, as it turns out.

Other incorrect answers judges come across are entertaining in a random sort of way. Our favorite wrong answer of the tournament comes in Round 4, when, instead of the correct EARLOBE for the clue "Stud's place," one contestant inexplicably writes in ESTONIA.

Round 5 is traditionally the most difficult puzzle of the tournament, and solvers expect a rough ride. But this year, buzz has begun to circulate that puzzle 5 is going to be especially painful, and, as the round is about to begin, I sense their anxiety.

"Puzzle #5 is a thirty-minute crossword constructed by Byron Walden," Shortz announces at the beginning of the round. The audience boos playfully, fearing what's to come, as Walden waves in acknowledgment. "He's really a nice guy," Shortz reminds the crowd, who laughs in response.

Thirty minutes later, they're not laughing. They're beaten, battered, and borderline pissed. Walden hides out in the Judges' Room, which is a smart move.

"I've been coming here for fifteen years, and I've never not completed a puzzle," solver Amy Goldstein tells me. "But I left about a third of this puzzle blank. I just had no idea."

"Is it really necessary to make a puzzle this difficult? What's the point?" another contestant pleads, without a hint of humor in her voice.

Veteran judge David Rosen says he can only remember one crossword in tournament history that was anywhere close to this, and it was a championship-round puzzle years ago.

The brutal numbers: of the 500 people in the room, only about fifty solve puzzle #5 in the allotted thirty minutes; of those fifty, only twenty-two complete it without an error.

What makes Walden's Round 5 crossword such a "bitch puzzle," as one contestant labels it? It isn't the theme. The puzzle's title is "XBOX," and its theme is an Ambrose Bierce quote scattered piecemeal around the grid, a standard crossword technique. Slightly unusual (but by no means unheard of) is Walden's trick of putting a circle in the four corner squares of the grid; as hinted at by one of the clues, these four circled squares spell KISS when the puzzle is correctly solved, and "kiss" is the word defined by the Bierce quote in the grid, taken from *The Devil's Dictionary* ("kiss: a word invented by the poets as a rhyme for bliss"). All in all, then, not an especially difficult theme, especially for Round 5.

The fill words are likewise not especially difficult, with a few exceptions. As is usual for Walden's grids, there are lots of lively phrases: TENNIS SHOE, PALE BLUE, IRISH PUB, and SEARCH ME, for instance. There are a few tough words in there, like PIAVE (a kind of Italian cheese no one has heard of), and OXANA (as in the not-especially-well-known Russian pianist Oxana Yablonskaya), but most crosswords have a tough little vocab, so, as with the theme, there is nothing notably difficult about the words in the grid, either.

What makes "XBOX" near-impossible to solve is one thing, and one thing only: the clues. Every crossword has a few tough clues, but this crossword has nothing *but* tough clues, most of them cloaking their answers through either misdirection or vagueness. FALSETTO is clued as "Pitched like a girl?"; SECRECY is "Some government employees work in it"; TEAMSTER is "Semi-conductor?"; ISLETS is "Minor keys"; THE NEWS is "Something to spread"; "Underground system" is SEWERS; and so on.

When working a puzzle, a top solver usually starts with a few easy-to-get words, just to gain a toehold in the grid. Vague or misdirecting clues like the ones above are usually glossed over with a mental "could be anything," and the solver moves on. This puzzle has an extraordinary amount of "could be anything" clues, though, which makes gaining a toehold very, very tough.

It is traditional on puzzle #5 for Shortz to announce, "One minute to go," and the audience to react with a brief groan. This year, when Shortz gives his sixty-second warning, the audience reacts with outright laughter, a few pieces of shouted commentary, and even a couple of near-screams. The noise doesn't die down for about thirty seconds, but nobody shushes anyone else; it's not like they're making any progress on the damn thing anyway. When the judges go around to collect the papers after Shortz calls time, about half the contestants hand their puzzles over face-down, so ashamed by the unfilled fields of white they've left that they don't want the collecting judges to see them.

Up in the Judges' Room, the officials grading puzzle 5 keep track of the record for papers with the fewest number of right answers. When I arrive from the tournament room their best is a puzzle with just 6 words filled in correctly. Soon a judge announces she's got a 5, then someone finds a 4 right after that, and soon we hit a 3, and then, amazingly, a 2. Imagine: in thirty minutes, a tournament solver got only two words correct in the entire puzzle.

Then, to our astonishment, judge Jim Page announces that he's got a 1. "No way," I call over to his table. "Let me see that." I glance over it and point out to Jim that he's mistaken —one of the few partially filled in (but mostly incorrect) sections of the grid actually conceals a second correct word, so this puzzle is a 2, not a 1.

"Oh, OK," Jim says, taking his paper back. "That's different. Two's really not so bad on this puzzle."

Saturday night's evening activity is twofold. First, a sudoku contest run by New Zealander Wayne Gould, the retired magistrate who ignited global sudoku mania by marching into the London *Times* unannounced and hooking their features editor on his addictive puzzle. Then, an advance screening of the documentary *Wordplay*, a surprise hit at the 2006 Sundance Film Festival about—well, about the American Crossword Puzzle Tournament.

It's clear right off the bat which of the two activities the audience is more psyched about. Though sudoku is popular with the general public, it gets the cold shoulder from some crossword constructors, and you can feel the chill in the room as Gould takes the stage, since many of the solvers in the tournament double as puzzle writers. He's introduced by Shortz but receives an almost embarrassingly tepid amount of applause. Fortunately he doesn't seem to notice, and launches into a somewhat odd, rambling two-minute discussion of whether the game is correctly spelled as one word ("sudoku"), two words, ("su doku"), or three words ("su do ku").

I find Gould charming in a professorial, absentminded genius sort of way, but his talk bombs with the crowd. "British Airways sent a memo around telling flight attendants not to solve sudoku during takeoffs and landings," he quips, but almost nobody laughs. I feel bad for the guy: following Ken Jennings as the evening entertainment emcee is a tall order.

Then the contest begins: judges pass out sheets to all 350 people in the ballroom (a large number of tournament entrants are noticeably absent). The sheets contain three puzzles, but the audience seems only mildly interested, even though Gould has told them this will actually turn out to be the largest sudoku competition that's ever been held. I notice that a few contestants decline to participate when a judge attempts to hand them a paper, and ace crossword solver Amy Reynaldo will later write on her weblog, "I was most of the way through the first one when I made some sort of error and said, 'Screw it. There's a bar in this hotel,' and went off to find socializing instead of sudokuing."

"There is a backlash against sudoku," puzzle maven Stan Newman asserts. That's not to say that sudoku isn't popular among cruciverbalists, because it is. "I don't solve crosswords anymore," top constructor Joe DiPietro tells me. "And for the first time in my life, if I am solving a crossword, I don't care about finishing it. I do care about finishing sudoku, though."

But there are also those who passionately hate the game. "Right when they started passing out sudoku, I headed for the bar," puzzle writer and math professor Rich Silvestri says (presumably he saw Reynaldo there). The reason for the backlash is two-fold. First, the artistic reason: some puzzle writers view sudoku as too easy, a mindless game you can practically brute-force a solution out of any time you want, like a word search.

This criticism isn't entirely fair, though, since sudoku, like crosswords, can be calibrated to very high levels of solving difficulty, and there is a certain mathematical elegance in the deep logic required to puzzle out certain areas of a well-made, tough sudoku puzzle.

The "they're too easy" argument masks the real reason for the backlash, which is resentment: many of us have spent serious chunks of our lives honing the craft of crossword puzzle writing, and along comes this computer-generated fad that's winning the hearts and minds of the masses. If everyone loves sudoku so much, who needs us anymore? With one click of his mouse, Gould—who provides his puzzles free to 400 papers around the world as a marketing plan to sell his sudoku-generating program—quite possibly entertains more people than all the crossword writers in this room combined. And his reach is international to a much greater degree than ours is; hence, the Kiwi's cool reception. Pity the successful; they pay for it somehow.

Even after people know who he is, I don't see very many

contestants dogging Gould the way they do Ken Jennings. In the Judges' Room—Gould is helping with officiating duties this year—few judges besides me make any attempt to engage him in conversation, which I find almost impolite, seeing as how the man has flown across the Pacific for this. Perhaps there isn't much to say; even acknowledging the game's beauty, one can't easily discuss a sudoku the way a crossword puzzle can be talked about. "I loved the theme of your crossword last week, and SPACE JAM was a really cool entry, and the clue to ZANZIBAR was tricky—" That's all standard crossword banter. But there is no such thing as sudoku banter—"figuring out that 6 in the upper right corner was tough . . ." just doesn't seem to cut it.

Shortz announces the winners of the contest, then hands out some checks and a few sudoku books as prizes. And then it's time for the main event of the evening, the event there's no backlash at all against: the screening of *Wordplay*.

It's the same chandeliered hotel ballroom the contestants have been solving puzzles in all day, but now it's been transformed into a 500-seat theater. I stuff my face too long out at the faux-movie concession stand, where the film's production company has sponsored a pre-screening eat session with open bar, soft pretzels, popcorn, and hot dogs, and when I finally make my way into the ballroom, chairs are scarce. I've just mentally resigned myself to not having a seat when a hotel employee appears with extra chairs, so I'm spared the long stand. People around me aren't so lucky. The house is jammed with humanity to the point where I find myself thinking semi-seriously about fire codes. Unlike the sudoku tournament, no one's crept off to the lobby bar for this.

Will Shortz introduces the film's director, Patrick Creadon, an outgoing, energetic midwesterner who'd attended the tournament last year, camera in tow. He and his wife (also the movie's producer) had spent the months before last year's tournament at the homes of eight contestants, getting a sense for how they trained for the upcoming competition. Featured were Al Sanders, who lost last year's final in shocking fashion, after absentmindedly calling out "Done!" before realizing he'd left two squares blank; perennial finalist Ellen Ripstein, whose memorable quote in the film is "I had this boyfriend who was always kind of putting me down. And I was just like, 'well, what are *you* the best in the country at?'; and beer swilling, frat boy genius Tyler Hinman, who won last year's tournament while a junior at Rensselaer. "Solving crossword puzzles takes what we call fluid intelligence," one of Hinman's IT professors intones; the next shot, wittily, is of the beer fridge in Hinman's fraternity house.

I'd remembered seeing Creadon at last year's event, filming everything, but hadn't thought much of it. I'd even helped out in a scene, where former champ Trip Payne needed to be filmed finishing a puzzle and having a judge come over to retrieve it from him (that was me). But I'd thought, "So they're making a documentary. And?" It wasn't the first time a documentary filmmaker had chronicled the tournament, after all.

But *Wordplay* took off. The Sundance Film Festival accepted it, and it received phenomenal reviews there, which virtually guaranteed it wide release throughout the country. This was only the second public screening of the film (the first being Sundance itself), and it was happening in the very room where much of the movie was shot. Way cool.

The movie is a hit with the audience, of course, since many of them are in it, either as featured players or as brief blips in crowd-panning shots. But subject matter aside, it's also a cleverly edited, witty, fun movie on its own merits. Creadon interviews celebrity crossword fans like Bill Clinton, pitching ace Mike Mussina, folk duo Indigo Girls, and comedian Jon Stewart (who, while solving a *New York Times* puzzle, notes a tricky clue and warns into the camera, "Don't get cute with me, Shortz. *Do not get cute with me.*")

Part of the film's appeal is its innovative use of graphics to sex up puzzle specifics for the viewer. In one scene, filmed at Al Sanders' Colorado home, Sanders is attempting to solve a crossword in less than two minutes at his kitchen table. The camera stays focused on the actual puzzle the entire time it's being solved (it actually takes Sanders two minutes and two seconds to finish, which seems to irritate him). But early on in the process the screen splits, and a graphic representation of the puzzle grid fills up with the letters Sanders is solving as he's writing them in. Who knew that watching a guy solve an entire crossword could be film-worthy? But it is.

The annual Saturday Night Beer Bash is a secret. It's mostly just judges allowed, but a few, select solvers are invited, too, by hosts Fred Piscop and Rich Silvestri. And you can definitely be uninvited, as one big-name constructor was several years back after having one too many and attempting to throw a TV through the hotel room window.

Piscop and Silvestri are microbrew-loving warhorses of the crossword scene, the kind of fiftysomething guys who've seen and done it all and have a realistic view of life and just want to have a little fun before it's all over. When I show up at this year's event there are about twenty people packed into their hotel room. "We made sure to get buffer rooms this year," Piscop tells me, meaning that the rooms on either side of theirs are people who'll be at the beer bash, which avoids noise complaints to the front desk. Piscop's demeanor reminds me of the Harry Shearer character from *This Is Spinal Tap*—he looks like he's had a pretty fun life thus far, and sports a T-shirt for a brand of beer called "Arrogant Bastard Ale."

No TVs head out the window, but cramped threesomes and foursomes talk shop and crowd on hotel beds as empty brown beer bottles—home brew, some of it—grow to dominate tabletops around the room. Round number 7 is at 9 AM, though, which makes midnight last call for most solvers in attendance. The group distills to about eight, and Peter Gordon, the *New York Sun* crossword editor, has had a bit much to drink. "This is the one night of the year I can get drunk," Gordon pleads when others give him a hard time. He's a family man with two full-time crossword jobs, so we cut him some slack.

Besides, he's really entertaining, and passionate about crossword puzzles. Every year at some point, the beer bash devolves into Peter holding court about puzzle themes, and we've arrived at that point now. "HIDEKI IRABU," Gordon bellows. "Do you know who he is? Do you know who he is?"

Sure, a few of us indicate. Yankees pitcher, late 1990s.

"OK. So notice his first name ends with I, and his last name starts with I. The puzzle I ran had five theme entries, and every one of them was a person whose first name ends with a vowel, and then the last name starts with that same vowel."

Gordon leans back in his chair grinning and takes another swig of beer, and it's understood that we're supposed to guess answers.

"Ursula Andress," I throw out.

"That would work," Gordon says, "but it's not the one I used. Anyway, the really tough one was IRABU. There aren't any other people with the I."

"I'm sure there are," I counter. "There have to be."

"There are *none*," Gordon declares, making a sweeping gesture with his arm, like he's clearing off a table. "I've got this database and there aren't any."

"So if I come up with one now, will you give me $20?"

"Yes. Definitely. There's no way."

Incentivized and confident, the group begins brainstorming. Not fifteen seconds later, David Rosen, who's reclined on one of the beds to think, springs up and claps his hands together. "Midori Ito!" he calls out. "The violinist!"

Gordon is stunned, but several people in the room confirm that Midori Ito is in fact a famous violinist, and he gamely forks over the $20. A minute later someone points out that the famous violinist is actually the one-named Midori, and Midori Ito is a figure skater, but it doesn't matter—the figure skater is famous enough, and the name works.

(Two days later, back at home, I'll find golfer JULI INKSTER via a websearch, and Gordon promises to give me $20 the next time we meet.)

We wind up guessing three of the other four names quickly—IRA ALLEN (brother of Ethan Allen; I've never heard of Ira, and neither has Will Shortz, apparently, who shakes his head in wonder when Rosen calls the name out); DALE EVANS, which bash host Rich Silvestri gets; and actor MILO O'SHEA (Rosen again). But the U has us stumped, even though we know the name must be eight letters long to balance out IRA ALLEN in the grid.

"There are 1-2-3-4-5-6-7 people in this room," Gordon pointlessly counts out, "and I bet six of you have never heard of this guy. He's a poker player." Someone finally comes up with STU UNGAR, whom I haven't heard of. Later I look him up and Ungar's a tough but legitimate crossword entry: he won the World Series of Poker's main event an unprecedented three times before dying of heart failure from years of cocaine abuse in 1998.

That challenge exhausted, Joe DiPietro calls out another one. A couple of brave tournament participants, including crossword blogger Amy Reynaldo, have joined the party, as has infamous Round 5 puzzle writer Byron Walden, so we're up to about ten again. DiPietro's query: what are the most hackneyed specific crossword themes? Not just theme ideas that have been used over and over again, he clarifies, but themes with specific entries?

Two pop out right away: ERNEST HEMINGWAY, A FAREWELL TO ARMS, and THE SUN ALSO RISES, three 15-letter theme entries that have appeared probably over

100 times in puzzles. Also with probable membership in the 100 or More Club is THE UNITED STATES, INDEPENDENCE DAY, STARS AND STRIPES, and THE FOURTH OF JULY. As with Hemingway, it's an obvious theme where all the entries are conveniently 15 letters long, so it's been used and overused a zillion times.

2:04 AM, the alarm clock reads. Piscop's body language couldn't be clearer—he's lying down on his bed with his eyes closed—so the last few hangers-on take the hint and skedaddle. Another ACPT Saturday Night Beer Bash draws to a close, and those who participated know that the morning hour will come all too soon—and with it, we'll find out the next day, scoring controversy.

Sunday morning, 8:15, the lobby. A little hungover, but not too bad. Tournament coordinator Helene Hovanec sees me before I see her, which means I won't have time to grab a Vanilla Coke from the gift shop. In her sweetest can-you-do-me-a-favor-but-you-don't-actually-have-a-choice tone she says, "Matt, we need you to help put the blinders up in the tournament room."

Round 7 will be starting in about thirty minutes, and 500 mustard-yellow anti-cheating blinders need to be set up on the tournament tables. It's one of the myriad mundane, easily forgettable tasks that have to be performed for an event like this, so I head over to the ballroom and grab a stack. About three-dozen contestants are scattered around the room, mostly practicing crosswords in anticipation of the round. I open each blinder and balance it on the table; between the beer last night and an inexplicably early 6:30

AM call from my girlfriend, I'm not in the best shape, so I'm happy for the solitary, repetitive, mindless task.

As I'm unfolding one of the blinders, I notice that someone has scrawled in pencil on it: "Will Shortz is a ____." When Stan Newman enters the room a few minutes later, I show him what I found, but Stan is a hard man to shock. "Must have been written after puzzle 5," he shrugs. "At least they didn't fill in the blank."

By 8:45 the updated scores for all 500 contestants are posted on a wall in the lobby. Entrants crowd and crane their necks to see where they stand. At the top of the leader board it looks like there aren't any surprises, and the three finalists are practically foreordained: Tyler Hinman, Ellen Ripstein, and Trip Payne—all former champs—are 1-2-3, and they're each at least three minutes ahead of the fourth-place competitor, Katherine Bryant. That's an awful lot of time to make up, and all three know they just have to play defensively to sail into the finals. Just solve quickly, but not carelessly, and make sure to take an extra minute to check their work if they need to. Also, they'll want to keep an eye on Katherine, making sure her hand doesn't go up extremely fast, like it did on Round 5's brutal puzzle, when she beat the entire room by an amazing two full minutes.

As the round begins, I'm playing hooky outside the tournament hall with two other judges. Technically we should be inside the ballroom waiting for raised hands, but the puzzle just got passed out, and I did all that blinder setting up besides, so Shortz can just deal with it: I'm taking a few minutes of Vanilla Coke time, dammit. The hotel gift shop was inaccessible before the round, crammed with contestants buying coffee and juice and candy. But now all those people are packed into a room seventy-five feet away, so the line went from "intolerable" to "nonexistent" in roughly three minutes' time.

Suddenly Trip Payne comes out of the tournament room, and he's not pleased. Payne takes the tournament more seriously than perhaps any other competitor; at the 2001 event, he stormed off in a huff when I made a mild joke about an error he'd made during a previous round. But taking it seriously has its rewards, since Payne has won the tournament three times.

Within earshot, Payne explains to Mike Shenk why he's mad. It turns out that he wasn't in third place after all going into Round 7, he was in fourth. Right after the scores were posted that morning, top solver Kiran Kedlaya approached Will Shortz to question what his error had been on puzzle #5. After a quick investigation, Kedlaya's error was reversed.

What had happened was this: Kedlaya had erased an incorrect word during the course of the tough Round 5 solve, and a stray erasure mark had turned into a nearby W into what appeared to be a blank square." The decision to reverse was clearly correct, since the intent of the solver is paramount, and it was clear upon a second look that Kedlaya hadn't intended to erase the W. Even if he had, a correctly filled in letter later erased is counted as correct if no other letter is written on top of it.

The scoring change means that Kedlaya has shot up to second place, which left Hinman in first, but put Ripstein in third, and, critically, Payne in fourth. "If I'd known I was in fourth, I wouldn't have played this round defensively," I hear Payne tell Shenk. Instead, he would have attempted to blaze through the puzzle, valuing speed over accuracy while hoping to solve clean (i.e. not make any mistakes).

Shenk, a tournament judge, takes in Payne's complaint and deadpans, "Well, for the right price, I can make sure Kiran has an error in Round 7."

That lightens the mood a bit. Payne later realizes that he probably couldn't have caught Kedlaya anyway, and though he wishes he'd known his standing beforehand, he's still sanguine. As he writes on his weblog after the tournament, "Let me make this clear: I'm happy that they fixed the mistake, and that Kiran was placed where he belonged; I would not have wanted to make the finals because of a bad ruling."

That's Stamford in a nutshell. Even the guy who takes it the most seriously doesn't need to win *that* badly.

After Round 7, Shortz announces the names of the nine finalists. There are actually three three-player final rounds: The A finals, which is the big enchilada to decide the overall tournament champion, but also lower B-and C-group finals for players who haven't finished above a certain level in the tournament before. The crowd goes nuts when (tournament rookie, in addition to being *Jeopardy!* champ) Ken Jennings is announced as a finalist in Group C.

I have an odd officiating duty for the finals: another judge and I are to chaperone the six A- and B-group finalists to a far-off, undisclosed location in the hotel while the C-group final is taking place, and then I alone will chaperone the A-group while the B-group final is contested. This is done because all three groups of finalists solve the same puzzle on the oversized grids before the audience; this year it's a

Mike Shenk brainbuster where the answer to 1-across, appropriately, is FINAL EXAM.

The catch is that although the answers in the grid are the same for all three finals groups, the clues given to finalists are different. The C Group's clues are the easiest, the B Group's clues get a little tougher, and the A Group's clues are downright nasty. Take the clue for 1-down, the answer to which is FUR COAT: for the C Group, it's defined fairly easily as "Garment put in summer storage"; for the B Group, it's toughened up to "Target of a paint-throwing activist"; while the A Group's clue is the practically ungettable "Hides in the closet."

Angst grips the six A- and B-Group finalists as they hide away in a basement corridor with their two chaperones, manifesting itself as pacing and idle chatter and trips to the water fountain while the minutes tick away. Despite being in the finals thirteen times previously, Ripstein later admits on her blog: "I was filled with nervous energy and went to the ladies' room even though I had gone not long before."

After a while a judge appears and announces that the B-Group final is ready to roll (Ken Jennings having won the C-Group final handily, as it turned out), which leaves me alone with Kedlaya, Hinman, and Ripstein. And I'm nervous.

I know all three of these people—Kedlaya beat me in the 1997 C-Group finals, in fact—and I have no real duties except standing here with them, yet I'm nervous to the point of sweating. Why? Because I've seen the solution for the final puzzle, and I'm afraid of ruining the entire tournament by accidentally blurting out a phrase or word from it. FINAL EXAM in particular is on my brain, so strongly that I feel I couldn't get some harmless phrase like "Good luck in the final" out without accidentally making it "Good luck on the final exam." Instead, I take Mark Twain's advice and keep my mouth shut, which works like a charm.

At last a judge appears to fetch the anointed trio, and they make their way to the ballroom. It's time to decide the 2006 champion.

Crossword great Merl Reagle and NPR's Neal Conan have the best seat in the house for the finals, a table right in front of the boards with a perfect view of all three finalists' puzzles. They need these seats since they're doing color commentary on the action for the audience of 600 (the three finalists wear noise-blocking headphones while solving so they can't hear Reagle and Conan's comments or answers blurted out by audience members). Assorted local media crowd the room along with the weekend's contestants.

The big digital clock is set at 15:00, and it's go time: the Group A final is underway. 14:59, 14:58, 14:57 . . .

After a couple of minutes they've each nailed down a modest number of entries, but all three have the incorrect STOP IT at 40-across instead of the correct DROP IT, an especially tough error to self-catch since it has so many letters in common with the right answer and appears to fit the clue ("Enough!") so perfectly. Hinman is the first to correct that error, but runs into generational trouble when he assumes that a five-letter word beginning with LOR and clued as "Co-star of five Bogart films" is Sophia LOREN instead of the correct Peter LORRE. This screws his corner up for about forty-five seconds, but Kedlaya and Ripstein have problems of their own. When frizzy-haired MIT math professor Kedlaya appears not to know that 7-down ("Quest's cousin") is the Nissan sport-utility model XTERRA, Neal Conan jokes to the crowd, "Do they even have SUV's at MIT?"

Ripstein stumbles on the same clue, putting in SIERRA. In the same corner Kedlaya provides the funniest wrong answer of the round: at 1-down, that diabolical "Hides in the closet" clue, Kedlaya has the O and the T of FUR COAT but hasn't hit upon the wordplay; in frustration, he enters ISN'T OUT into the grid, which the audience roars at. It fits, but it's wrong. Later he conquers the corner by getting both this clue and the other major stumper in the area: at 15-across the answer UNO, DUE, TRE, which is evilly clued as "Count of Monte Cristo."

The final result is a blowout: Hinman finishes the puzzle with no mistakes using eleven minutes and thirty-one seconds. Kedlaya and Ripstein fail to complete the puzzle in the allotted fifteen minutes, but Kedlaya takes second place with three errors to Ripstein's seven.

"Last year wasn't a fluke," Will Shortz jokes, as he proclaims Hinman the winner of the 2006 tournament. The crowd applauds, and seems to sense that it won't be the last time. The margin of this year's victory, when combined with Hinman's win the previous year and his extreme self-confidence, give the distinct sense that we're at the beginning of an era.

CHAPTER 2

Inextricably Linked

There is one, and only one, rock star–level celebrity in crosswords: Will Shortz.

Instead of me describing it to you in fuzzy terms, let's quantify Shortz's fame precisely in the modern way. Googling "Will Shortz" and "crossword puzzle" yields 141,000 hits. The next greatest number I can find for a puzzle person's name + "crossword puzzle" is 22,000 (Stanley Newman). Therefore, we might reasonably say that Shortz is about six-and-a-half times as famous as the next person in crosswords. Even that number may understate his case: when people at parties find out what I do for a living, "Do you know Will Shortz?" is a common follow-up question. Nobody else is asked about. Ever.

Shortz generates an astonishing amount of media coverage. In addition to the *Wordplay* documentary, he's been featured in his own *60 Minutes* segment, made appearances on shows like *Martha Stewart Living* and CNN's *Morning Edition*, and been profiled in newspapers and magazines like the *Wall Street Journal*, the *Chicago Tribune*, and

Newsweek. Bill Clinton sent him a note for his fiftieth birthday. You get the idea; the guy is famous.

More than a mere celebrity, though, Will Shortz is also a brand. His *New York Times* crossword books sell great, but is that because it's the *Times* brand or because it's the Will Shortz brand? The sudoku craze gave us a controlled experiment to address that question, and the answer came back that the Shortz name clearly has something to do with it: Shortz's six books of sudoku sold over 200,000 copies in the week before Christmas in 2005, and one of those six was the top-selling sudoku book in the nation that same year.

They were books of high quality, to be sure, but high-quality sudoku are easy to have a computer churn out, and anyone could have put out a book of them (and many did, including me). But in a suddenly popular field with no established gurus, Shortz's name, emblazoned in huge print on the books' covers, was the brand that converting crossword fans flocked to in droves. People, it turns out, want frozen pizzas with the name Wolfgang Puck on the box, jackets with the name Giorgio Armani on the label, and puzzle books with the name Will Shortz on the cover.

He'd had big-name jobs before he became puzzle editor at the *New York Times*: editor of *GAMES Magazine*, Puzzlemaster on NPR's *Weekend Edition*, director of the American Crossword Puzzle Tournament. But it was the *Times* gig that launched Shortz into actual superstardom, so the man and the newspaper are now inextricably linked in the public's mind. It makes sense to tell the story of Shortz, then, by first telling the story of the *Times* and its crossword.

● ● ●

If you want to be taken seriously as a crossword puzzle writer, you must get published in the *New York Times*. There's really no way around it. You can write a puzzle for a good daily like the *Los Angeles Times*, or a quality niche magazine like *GAMES World of Puzzles*, or even syndicate your own crosswords out to newspapers and Web sites across the country, and that'll be great—but to the average person, it won't matter. Their eyes will only light up in recognition and respect if you can say you've had a puzzle byline in the Gray Lady.

In *Wordplay*, talk show host Jon Stewart quips that no other crossword is quite like the *Times*': "I'll do the *USA Today* puzzle if I'm in a hotel or on a plane," he explains, "but I won't feel good about myself." Fans of the puzzle feel the same way: solving a different crossword would be like having a rum and Coke made with RC Cola—even if you like RC Cola, you're still not drinking a real rum and Coke. TV ads for the *New York Times* home delivery service make a point of featuring the puzzle, and the very words "*New York Times* crossword puzzle" carry a ring and a gravitas that "*Chicago Tribune* crossword puzzle," for example, simply doesn't.

Some of this is just branding and the comfort of a familiar product. If you gave a rum and Coke drinker a rum and RC without telling him, there's a fair chance he wouldn't notice the difference, and the *New York Times* could run *Los Angeles Times* puzzles for a week without anyone calling them on it. Or longer, perhaps: in the years before Shortz took over in 1993, many knowledgeable critics didn't even feel that editor Eugene T. Maleska's *New York Times* puzzles were even any good, much less the best in the country, yet the puzzle's reputation did not suffer appreciably from a wider cultural (or financial) point of view.

And there are other puzzles besides the *Times* with fan bases, to be sure. With his trademark wacky puns, Merl Reagle has self-syndicated to a devoted audience over the past thirty years in papers like the *San Francisco Examiner* and the *Philadelphia Inquirer*, while rival hipster constructors Matt Jones and Ben Tausig have each syndicated their way to a name in the edgy alternative weekly market.

Those are quirky weekly crosswords, not daily staples like the *Times*, but there are other good, mainstream daily puzzles as well. Besides the *Los Angeles Times*, both *Newsday* and a peer-edited constructor group called CrosSynergy turn out good-quality daily puzzles that might not make Jon Stewart suffer too badly while solving. The *New York Sun* puzzle, as we'll see later in the chapter, has even begun nipping closely at the *Times*' heels in terms of overall quality. So, despite what Stewart says, a solver deprived of his daily *New York Times* crossword isn't necessarily forced into slumming elsewhere with a lousy puzzle.

And yet the *Times* crossword is special, for a number of reasons. First, it boasts the heft of history, having debuted in 1942 and gained its reputation under Margaret Farrar, the editor who shaped the *Times* puzzle—and American crosswords in general—during its first twenty-seven years. A twenty-five-year-old woman today may solve the *New York Times* puzzle as part of her daily routine, knowing that her mother and grandmother did the same thing in the same paper when they were her age.

It is also the most widely syndicated crossword in the country, printed in 150 papers during the week and 300 on Sundays. Obviously being popular and far-reaching is a good thing in and of itself, but it's also important for quality's sake, since a constructor who comes up with an especially brilliant idea for a puzzle is likely to give the *Times* first crack at it, if only for exposure's sake.

Speaking in strict terms of quality, the *Times* has been the best puzzle in the country for most of its sixty-four years. Though rivals occasionally rise to challenge it, sometimes successfully, the *Times* crossword has been pretty consistently at or near the top of the quality heap since the FDR Administration.

Finally, the *Times* is fortunate to have Will Shortz as their puzzle's current editor, as his affability and skill, with both puzzles and people, has turned him into the first true crossword celebrity, a status which reflects well upon the paper that hired him thirteen years ago. And celebrity here is not just fluff: bringing the *Times* crossword off the page and into real life enhances solvers' enjoyment of the puzzle in meaningful ways. Lots of *Times* puzzle fans know Shortz through his media appearances and view the crossword as a highly personal, Me vs. Shortz battle of wits; outsmarting the Puzzlemaster, or being outsmarted by him, is a critical sliver of their day.

No institution is perfect. There are legitimate criticisms to be made of the *Times* crossword, both historically and contemporarily, and I will make them later in this chapter. But the *Times* puzzle is indisputably outstanding, and dear to the hearts of an enormous number of solvers, and it holds a secure and unique place in the country's cultural landscape.

It is, after all, the *New York Times* crossword puzzle.

Margaret Petherbridge was born in New York City in 1897 and died there as Margaret Petherbridge Farrar in 1984. The time in between these two events she spent becoming the most important person in American crossword puzzle history.

Don't take my word for it, look at her résumé: In 1920, she became editor of the *New York World* crossword (the *World* being the newspaper in which Arthur Wynne published the first crossword ever in 1913). In 1924, she co-edited the first crossword puzzle book ever published, Simon & Schuster's *The Cross Word Puzzle Book*. That book became Volume #1 in a series she edited or co-edited until her death; the final volume to carry her byline was #136. And, in 1942, she was tapped to be the first editor of the *New York Times* crossword.

At that time, those words meant little. As the story goes, *Times* publisher Arthur Hays Sulzberger was tired of having to buy rival papers to get his crossword fix, so he brought the well-respected Farrar on to make the fledgling *Times* puzzle better than the competition's.

Farrar is the person most responsible for standardizing the rules that make American crossword puzzles what they are today: no more than one-sixth of the puzzle grid can be filled by black squares; grids must have "180-degree rotational symmetry," meaning that when the puzzle is turned upside-down the pattern of black squares remains unchanged; each entry must be a minimum of three letters in length; and every letter in the grid must be part of both an across and a down word, in order to give the solver two chances at each letter.

As Abner Doubleday codified the rules of baseball, Margaret Farrar codified the rules of crosswords. Without rules there can be no beauty, so her influence reaches into every crossword puzzle written in the past six decades.

Farrar also standardized rules about taste, and placed unprecedented focus on the quality of the solver's experience. As Merl Reagle wrote in a 1997 *Philadelphia Inquirer* piece:

> I still have that first letter I got back from Margaret when I was sixteen. In it she tells why two of the puzzles I submitted were unacceptable . . . One had DEAD AS A DOORNAIL and ROTTEN IN DENMARK—"not very pleasant terms." The second puzzle had EDEMA [accumulation of fluid in bodily tissues] and RALE ("that's the death rattle, not very pleasant either"). She wrote, "Crosswords are an entertainment. Avoid things like death, disease, war and taxes—the subway solver gets enough of that in the rest of the paper." . . . Entertainment? Subway solver? These ideas had never entered my puny head.

In the 1950s, Farrar also published the first crossword to have a recognizable theme. She would later help standardize rules on this subject as well, such as theme words having to be placed symmetrically in the grid.

Between her focus on the solver's enjoyment of the puzzle, her hand in molding the shape and structure of the American crossword puzzle form, and the overall high quality of the puzzles she published in the paper, it was Farrar's twenty-seven-year tenure that imbued the words "*New York Times* crossword puzzle" with much of the meaning they still carry today.

When Farrar was forced by *Times* age restrictions to retire in 1969, she was succeeded by Will Weng, a character who edited to mostly favorable reviews until 1977. At that point, the *New York Times* crossword was clearly the best daily puzzle in the country, as it had been under Farrar. Like Farrar, Weng generally stressed innovation and fun and the solver's pleasure. Under Weng's successor Eugene T. Maleska, however, the situation became somewhat more complex.

In *The Story of Language*, Mario Pei writes of a language teacher he knew: "One former colleague of mine used literally to dance with glee every time he was able to find an obscure rule or word on which he could stick his pupils in an exam. He utterly forgot the purpose of language teaching."

Harsh though it may sound, the same might be said about Maleska (who also happened to be a language teacher). He intentionally had the *New York Times* crosswords filled with "crosswordese"—rare, obscure words not even a well-educated solver could possibly be expected to know. As a result, some critics felt that the *Times* puzzle, during Maleska's tenure, ceased to be the best crossword in the country; on many days, they said it wasn't even a decent puzzle, and often it was downright unfair, overflowing pointlessly with unabridged dictionary-only words like ANOA (an Indonesian ox) and ANI (a kind of blackbird) and ESNE (a medieval serf). It was as if, in contrast to Farrar and Weng, Maleska had almost an adversarial relationship with solvers.

In his book *Cruciverbalism*, Stanley Newman recounts an infamous example of a Maleska clue, what Newman terms "the Loa Outrage":

> Now, in the course of building a crossword puzzle, it is sometimes necessary to include the sequence L-O-A when you've got an exquisite stack of words that will work only if you can keep those three letters in the mix. Fair enough. The painless tradition is to give the clue "Mauna ___," for the famous volcano in Hawaii, and move on. No doubt *Times* puzzle editor Eugene Maleska wanted to find a fresh way of cluing LOA. But "Seat of Wayne County, Utah" was beyond the pale. Aside from the 364 residents of Loa, Utah, at the time (I looked it up) and possibly a few cross-country truck drivers, it was unlikely that anyone who sat down with the *Times* puzzle that day would have known the three-letter answer to the Wayne County clue.

Maleska was by most accounts a gruff man who often veered into outright hostility, though even his detractors admit he had a gentle side. In Coral Amende's *The Crossword Obsession*, puzzle writers tee off on the late *Times* puzzle editor, recounting their most horrific Maleska experiences. Liz Gorski relates how she got a rejection letter from Maleska that began, "I'm sick and tired of your puzzles."

"He went on," Gorski says, "to describe my work in superlative terms—my puzzles were some of the worst he had ever seen . . . confused and saddened, I threw in the towel on constructing puzzles."

Today, Gorski is one of the top crossword writers in the country. The overall effect of Maleska's hostility to puzzle writers was to winnow down the pool of quality constructors who were willing to submit puzzles to the paper, another reason for the *Times* puzzle's fall from greatness during the Maleska years.

Maleska supporters—and there are a few—respond that while he had his faults, "Gene" could also be a supportive and encouraging editor, and that he did provide his share of innovation, such as the Stepquote, a type of theme where a quotation begins at the upper-leftmost square in the grid and winds its way down to the lower-rightmost. Granting that Maleska had his moments of kindness and positivity, it must be noted that the Stepquote is almost never seen in crosswords today, and is therefore not an innovation that lasted.

Around the beginning of Maleska's term, American crossword puzzles began to undergo a sea change. *GAMES Magazine* was launched in 1977, and the careers of up-and-coming young crossword writers like Henry Hook, Merl Reagle, Mike Shenk, and Stan Newman began to take off. These cruciverbalists spearheaded what came to be known as the "New Wave" in crossword constructing: their puzzles teemed with pop culture references, wicked humor, and nutty themes, all of which appealed to a somewhat younger and hipper audience. Newman even went so far as to label these young turks the "Anti-Maleskas."

How you felt about these changes depended largely upon how old you were: if you were in your fifties or sixties, say, and had been solving largely pop cultureless puzzles your whole life, you were quite possibly less than thrilled with crosswords that suddenly appeared with names of contemporary sitcoms and comedians and songs you'd never heard of. He may have been tough and even unfair at times, but overall, you may have liked Maleska just fine.

If you were in your twenties or thirties, and listened to this music and watched these movies and TV shows, you were probably more favorably inclined to finding them in your crossword puzzle. Since the people at *GAMES* were the twenties and thirties types, the magazine's growing influence began to change the kind of crossword puzzle many solvers liked and expected. Struggling through a Maleska-style puzzle full of obscurities and head-scratching arcana just wasn't much fun after you'd worked through a witty, celebrity laden, outrageously clued Henry Hook puzzle.

Maleska's tenure from 1977 to 1993 pretty much marked the slow decline of crosswordese-filled puzzles, as solvers and constructors gradually moved over to the New Wave camp. Even among older solvers some converts had been won, and ever-younger puzzle constructors (like yours truly) jumped happily aboard the New Wave ship. These brash crossword puzzles were not only fun and exciting to solve, they were fun and exciting to write.

In actuality, the *New York Times* crossword's brand suffered little with the general public during Maleska's years. There were enough older solvers who still preferred Maleska's style to keep the feature strong, and even many casual younger solvers weren't aware of the New Wave vs. Maleska debate going on. This was a pre-Internet era, a time when such niche arguments took place only in rant-filled pamphlets like Rich Silvestri's *CROSSW RD* or Stan Newman's *Crossworder's Own Newsletter* (peak circulation: 5,000). These movements in thought, then, shifting as they were in favor of the Anti-Maleskas, were largely off the radar of all but the most committed solvers.

Still, when Maleska passed away in 1993 and the *Times* needed to find his replacement, the paper's brass were aware that they needed someone to rejuvenate the puzzle. "They wanted someone who was younger but could span the generations," Shortz says. Of the three editors who applied, Shortz was indeed the youngest, and that, combined of course with his impressive resume, tilted the scales in his favor. It didn't hurt that Shortz was in good with an older generation of constructors, like Frances Hansen and Mel Taub, who had influence at the paper in picking Maleska's successor.

Times executive Jack Rosenthal knew of this group and, as final decision maker on the new hire, followed their advice in choosing Shortz. "Will Shortz was born to edit the *New York Times* Crossword," Rosenthal later said. The same might have been said five decades prior about Farrar.

It was Shortz's job, then, to both keep the remaining Maleska solvers happy—and there were (and perhaps still are) plenty of them—and also to nudge the *Times* crossword towards the New Wave and attract a wider audience to the puzzle. In this he has been largely successful. He got a lot of irate letters in his first few years, but they abated after a while. Some of these solvers wound up liking the Shortzian take on the New Wave after all, and others just stopped writing. But overall, a fair assessment of Shortz's thirteen-year tenure is that it has cemented the *Times* crossword's reputation at a moment when the brand was vulnerable to competition due to the stasis of the Maleska era.

I visit Will Shortz at his home in Pleasantville, New York, on a sharp, clear day in early January 2006. Though I've never been to it before, I've heard about his house many times, since it's famous in puzzles as the home of the largest collection of puzzle books and magazines in the world—some 20,000 volumes, including many in foreign languages.

Shortz has come down with a cold, but gamely declines to postpone the interview to a later date when I offer. After a Keystone Kops–worthy miscommunication about where at the train station he'll pick me up (made worse by my stalwart refusal to carry a cell phone), we eventually find each other and make the short drive to his home.

I first met Shortz at a crossword tournament in Baltimore in 1987, and have corresponded with him a fair amount (mostly while submitting crosswords to him for the *Times*) and seen him on perhaps eight occasions in the intervening nineteen years. As I have observed it, and as is echoed by his reputation in the puzzle world, Shortz's demeanor is calm and polite, generally putting at ease those he converses with. He is warm and pleasant to be around, though when I am around him, I've never been able to shake the notion that I'm in the presence of a famous person whose time is valuable. He possesses a kind of quiet charisma that I've only observed in a few people in my life, a star power that makes people want to win his approval. I suppose all celebrities may have this, and perhaps this intangible aura is how Shortz came to find himself among their ranks.

Physically, Shortz is a handsome man in his early fifties, a shade under 5'10", with dark brown hair, thinning just a bit these days, but not too much. He has worn a mustache for all his adult life and has a broad, kind smile that he shows frequently. He is in good shape primarily due to his passion for table tennis, a sport he engages in five or six nights a week at an average clip of three hours per night.

His Tudor-style house is located on a quiet, suburban street, and reminds me of my late grandmother's place: hardwood floors, nice old-timey door handles and bathroom fixtures, spare but elegant wooden décor. Once we enter, Shortz immediately pulls out an old-fashioned skeleton key and opens a locked glass cabinet by the front door. Inside are the most prized items from his mammoth collection, including a copy of the first crossword puzzle book ever printed (Farrar's aforementioned *The Cross Word Puzzle Book*, co-edited with Prosper Buranelli and F. Gregory Hartswick). It's the only copy Shortz knows of that lives outside a library.

Another prized possession kept under lock and key is an elegant black-and-white crossword puzzle bracelet from 1924, the era of the original crossword craze. Shortz was able to date the bracelet after finding an advertisement for it in a contemporary magazine.

After a few minutes with the glass cabinet, we sit down on the sofa to begin the interview, and then the phone rings in the kitchen. It won't be the first time. I mentioned that Shortz is a celebrity, and celebrity phones—well, they tend to ring.

Shortz sits back down after a few minutes, and I manage to get one question out before the phone rings again. The Puzzlemaster rises apologetically with the words "just a second, I need to take this," and disappears.

"Uh-huh . . . uh-huh . . ." I hear from around the corner. "Is that a morning show? We could do a giant grid . . . Right."

"I'm really sorry," Shortz assures me upon his return. "It's not usually this busy."

I believe the first half of that, but twenty minutes in we're still on his childhood in Indiana since he's already fielded a total of four calls (three setting up media appearances, the other from Helene Hovanec, Shortz's right-hand woman in organizing the ACPT). The breaks give me plenty of time—like, too much time—to review the questions I'd prepared for Shortz, including a few last-minute ideas I jotted down on the train ride ("Pounded the pavement early to get gigs?"; "Ever a time during career when considered getting out of puzzles?").

I get to ask a few of these questions, but then we're

interrupted again, and Shortz gives me another what-can-you-do shrug. And what can you do? Celebrity phones ring.

"I can't do it now because there's a writer at my house," I hear from the kitchen. "Yes . . . Correct . . . No, the best times for me would be Tuesday afternoon, like I said, or Friday afternoon, since I'm already in the city."

Shortz wasn't born in a city, but in a town: Crawfordsville, Indiana, in August of 1952. His mother was a homemaker and his father a personnel director. Standard stuff, but nonstandard was where they chose to raise Shortz and his sister: on a fifty-acre farm with eighteen Arabian horses. The family was a typical Midwestern ethnic mix, his late father's side of German stock and his mother's ancestry English and French.

Shortz first caught the solving bug when his mom gave him a puzzle book to keep him quiet while her bridge club was meeting. He was eight or nine years old, and by eighth grade he was hooked enough to write a paper for school stating that he wanted to be a professional puzzle maker when he grew up.

The eighth grader with a dream became the college freshman with a plan: at Indiana University, he earned an undergraduate degree in "enigmatology," the study of puzzles (Shortz is still the only person he knows of with this major). He'd found the word in an old dictionary and convinced enough department heads that it was a legit field of study to get a green light. His parents still insisted on law school after that, which Shortz attended at the University of Virginia.

"I realized in my first spring of law school that I did not want to pursue a career in law," Shortz tells me. Mom and Dad wouldn't take no law degree for an answer, though, so Shortz plowed through to a UVA J.D.

Having fulfilled his obligation to the parental units, Shortz looked after Charlottesville for an entry into working in the puzzle world. During summers at the law school grind he'd done stints at Penny Press, a puzzle magazine company in Connecticut. "I still thought I'd be a lawyer eventually," Shortz says. "Penny Press was just a summer job."

But some summer jobs turn year-round, and Shortz received an offer from Penny Press in 1977 to work there full time. At a salary of $10,000 a year, Shortz had his first full-time employment in puzzles. He had just turned twenty-five years old.

When the new, exciting puzzle magazine *GAMES* started up in 1978, Shortz landed a job there, and stayed full time from 1978 to 1990, including the last two years as the magazine's editor. In 1987, he got a gig on NPR as their weekly Puzzlemaster, a hugely popular radio segment that continues to this day (he gives an on-air series of word puzzles to call-in contestants, who win prizes playing by Shortz's quizzes).

In 1990 *GAMES* folded after a glorious twelve-year run, and the puzzle stars who worked there—Shortz, Mike Shenk, Henry Hook, and many others—scattered to the four winds, suddenly without a magazine to call home. But after a year, *GAMES* was bought and reintroduced under a slimmer, more freelance author-heavy format, and Shortz went back to work as its editor. Disputes with the new

owners led to Shortz and the magazine parting company in
early 1993, but Shortz landed on his feet; the crossword
puzzle world had just learned the news of Eugene T.
Maleska's death, and by now, the reader will know who
replaced him.

The New York Times crossword puzzle gets edited upstairs in
a small office and a larger library that doubles as a second
workspace. I really like the small office: it's about 12 x 15
feet, with white plaster walls, a crossword clock hanging on
one of them, and a little window looking out onto the street.

This room is where Shortz keeps his reference books,
about 250 in total. They range from books you'd naturally
expect a crossword editor to have (dictionaries, atlases,
almanacs, a giant Shakespeare concordance) to odd
sounding but clearly useful titles (*The Thesaurus of Slang,
Number One Country Hits*) to bizarrely-titled tomes I can
scarcely believe exist (*The Reverse Dictionary of Present
Day English* is my favorite, which is just like a normal dictionary, but with the entries spelled and listed backwards.
ZZUF (that's "fuzz") is the first entry in the book, for
example. When I seem confused by the book's reason for
being, Shortz intones conspiratorially, "For code-
breaking").

Shortz's editing process begins in this small home office
when he receives a puzzle from a constructor. He gets about
seventy-five submissions per week but can only use seven,
so the vast majority of puzzles get a rejection letter oozing
Hoosier kindness to ease the blow. No Maleska, this guy: I
remember receiving rejections from Shortz that were so nice

I had to read them twice to be sure he was actually passing on the puzzle.

Once a crossword's been moved into the yes pile, Shortz checks the grid for any sloppy areas that need to be cleaned up; perhaps an unpleasant entry of the EDEMA or RALE ilk that has to be surgically removed, or an accidental repeated entry in the grid that has to be changed (it's fairly common for a constructor to let a little word like ATE or ERE slip into a puzzle twice, especially in a larger puzzle). If the grid fix is major, Shortz might send it back to the constructor to patch up and resubmit.

Once the grid looks clean, it's on to the clues. Shortz changes roughly half the constructor's clues in any given puzzle in order to reach a desired difficulty level or otherwise punch them up in some way. Shortz tends to add a lot of pun-based stuff; I recall a *Times* puzzle of mine from the mid-1990s where he improved a boring clue I'd written for OCTOPI ("Sea threats") by making a crafty pun out of it ("Army threats?"—as in, "threats with many arms." On especially punny clues like this, Shortz, like most editors, will often append a question mark to warn the solver that wordplay lurks about).

After the clues are finalized and fact-checked using those 250 reference books, the puzzles go off to a quartet of test-solvers, three of whom are former ACPT champs. They make sure the puzzle's not way too hard or way too easy and do a final scan for errors. A thumbs up from this foursome sends the puzzles off to the paper, and voila—a *New York Times* crossword puzzle unto this Earth is born.

Entering the library next door is like stepping into a

pharaoh's tomb; I'm blinded and awed by the riches that surround me. The room itself is a bright, airy space with a computer workstation in the middle, but the first thing you notice is the four long walls groaning with puzzle books and magazines: over here, a stack of puzzle mags from the 1930s; over there, a shelf featuring crossword books in Hungarian; in this corner, the entire Simon & Schuster puzzle book series, dating from 1924 to the present; in that corner, a collection of Latin language riddles published in Frankfurt in 1545 (entitled *Aenigmatum Libri III*, or *Three Books of Riddles*).

We spend about twenty minutes in the room, which is, for me, like taking one gulp of water from a cold, pristine brook: enough for now, but I really wish I could carry this room around with me and partake of it at my leisure.

Back downstairs, I have time for just a couple more questions for my host. First, has Shortz noticed any change in the age of constructors since he took over?

"There are a lot more young constructors now," he says. "I've published ten or twelve teenagers in the *Times*, which is great."

What percentage of the *Times* puzzles are constructed with the help of a computer?

"I never ask," Shortz says. "But I can tell sometimes, if a constructor I've never seen suddenly submits a very wide-open grid." Shortz frowns on newbie constructors taking the computer shortcut, however, since he feels "they should have the skills to do the grid without the computer first, like an apprenticeship." That's how I did it, so while I realize that computers may be on the move (see Chapter 6), I like Shortz's answer.

My train is coming soon and the Puzzlemaster's cold is catching up with him, so it's time for me to go. Later I'll realize that I forgot to request a viewing of the famous crossword puzzle pinball machine in the basement.

"Come back anytime," Shortz tells me. For a crossword pinball machine and another look at that library, I probably will.

No one's life is without challenges—not mine, not yours, and, as it turns out, not Will Shortz's.

The Jamaican bobsled team tried to win a gold medal off the Austrians, Oracle wants to kick Microsoft to the curb, and everyone knows how David went fearlessly after Goliath. No matter how big and powerful you get, there's always going to be some upstart little guy who thinks he can take you down. We humans have many poor qualities, but this scrappiness in the face of long odds is one of our wonderful, redeeming ones. And the crossword puzzle world has its own little David: since 2002, there has been a daily crossword editor whose goal has actually been to make his newspaper's puzzle better than the *New York Times* crossword. Sounds a little crazy, but the interesting part is that he's making progress.

You'd probably never heard of him before reading the first chapter of this book, and maybe never heard of his paper: Peter Gordon is the editor, and the *New York Sun* is his medium. The *Sun* is a small but deep-pocketed Manhattan newspaper that was launched in 2002. Gordon, who used to work as a sub-editor for Shortz at the *Times*, jumped ship when the *Sun* began publishing, with the goal of making the new paper's puzzle the best in the country.

Again, this sounds ridiculous at first—how do you make a daily crossword better than the *Times*, especially with Shortz at the helm?—but a missionary zeal, combined with an almost surreal passion for crosswords, has served the forty-year-old Gordon well. Though not well-known outside of hardcore puzzle circles, his crossword is now generally considered the equal of the *Times* within these circles, and presents Shortz with a major challenge for the next few years of his tenure at the *Times*.

There are about a dozen daily puzzles across the land, and some of them are good; but before 2002, none of them were really in the same class as the *Times*, and none of them really tried to be. In the case of the *Newsday* and CrosSynergy daily puzzles, only a limited number of constructors contribute, so no matter how skilled those constructors are, they can't compete qualitywise with a freelance system that cherry-picks the very best puzzles from the 100-plus writers the *Times* uses. In the case of the *Los Angeles Times*, the pay is much lower than that of the *New York Times*, so constructors generally send their best work to Shortz first; if he rejects a puzzle, it might then be sent to the *Los Angeles Times* for consideration.

But the *Sun* puzzle is different in important ways, and these differences make it the only true rival to the *Times*; in a nutshell, there are several good daily puzzles in the U.S., but only two truly great ones.

First, the *Sun* attempts to be as difficult to solve as the *Times*—even more difficult, in fact—which the others don't (difficulty is not necessarily an indication of quality, but it's still interesting that *Sun* puzzles tend to be a bit tougher than

Times puzzles). A typical day on Amy Reynaldo's blog will list the *Sun* as the puzzle that took her the longest to solve, followed by the *New York Times*, then the *Los Angeles Times*, and CrosSynergy. It doesn't always work out in that pat order, but that's the most common sequence. Her solution times for February 2006, for example, she lists as:

NYS 6:00
NYT 5:30
LAT 3:38
CS 3:12

On occasion, the *Sun*'s puzzles are *much* more difficult to solve than the competition's: the next day's post lists her "NYT" solving time as 5:17, and her "NYS" time as 14:30, to which Reynaldo appends a parenthetical "ouch." Reynaldo finished in fifth place out of 500 entrants at the 2006 ACPT, so a daily-size puzzle that takes her fourteen minutes and thirty seconds to solve is roughly the level of the championship final-round puzzle at Stamford. Ouch, indeed; one valid criticism of Gordon's *Sun* puzzles is that they're just too damn hard, which a certain breed of solver won't recognize as a valid criticism, but the average solver probably will.

The *Sun* puzzle is also able to attract top constructors' work away from the *Times* because it pays more than the *Times* puzzle: $136 to the *Times*' $135. Behind these odd figures hangs a humorous tale that illustrates the rivalry: Gordon decided when he started his new puzzle that the *Sun* would be the highest paying market for daily puzzles, and beat the *Times* $75 rate by offering $90 per crossword (yes, that's how little papers pay for puzzles—more on that in a moment). The *Times* responded a few months later by matching Gordon's rate. Six minutes—you heard right, six minutes—after Shortz announced the *Times* increase on the main crossword puzzle listserv, Gordon posted that the *Sun*'s rate would be jumping to $95.

The comical jousting continued: the *Times* raised to $100 a few months later, and Gordon re-raised to $101, a figure the *Times* did not feel the need to match for a while, which allowed Gordon to keep claiming that he paid top dollar (literally, since he was on top by a dollar).

Two years later, in June of '05, Shortz got the *Times* to jump to $125, and then, sensing a coup de grace when Gordon didn't respond, the *Times* re-raised themselves to $135 a few months later. Could David counter Goliath's two successive substantial increases?

David could, and did. Gordon announced in April 2006 that the *Sun*'s new rate will be—you guessed it—$136, which is where the battle stands now. I await expectantly the next increase to $137, or perhaps $136.50 if money is tight.

Although the figures are small and the differences between the figures even smaller, the *Sun*'s constant increase of writer's fees does indicate a certain respect for crossword constructors on behalf of their management that seems rather lacking at the *Times*. I think constructors sense that, and sometimes send Gordon their best work because of it. This has nothing to do with the editors, but rather with the management who makes financial decisions at the two papers. If they could, I'm sure both Shortz and Gordon would love to pay constructors $500 or $1,000 per puzzle, but they are constrained by what their newspapers will give them. Still, the constructors understand that if not for gadfly Gordon's agitation, the *Times* might still be paying $75 per crossword, and he gets some appreciation from them on this point.

So which puzzle is better, the *Sun* or the *Times*? In the summer of 2005, I conducted an experiment that became an article in the *Weekly Standard*, which was labeled "New York's Crossword Wars" on the magazine's cover. The *casus belli* was this simple question: what's the best daily crossword puzzle in the country? To answer it, I decided to stage a competition between the *Sun* and *Times*, generally considered to be the best two daily puzzles in the land.

Judging any kind of art is tricky and subjective, but there are technical aspects to crosswords, like the undesirable existence of crosswordese, that can be measured with a certain degree of objectivity. In my survey for the *Standard* I solved fifty-six puzzles, half from the *Sun* and half from the *Times*, and assigned scores based on artistry and technical merit. My long-suffering girlfriend had the task of printing the puzzles out from the papers' Web sites and blacking out the titles and copyrights; this left me solving and scoring without knowing which paper's puzzles were which, to avoid any unconscious bias on my part one way or the other.

To my surprise, the *Sun* came out slightly ahead in the end, 432 points to 419 points based on the scoring system I had devised. Perhaps more interestingly, of the twelve puzzles from those fifty-six that I'd flagged as being especially clever in some way, eight were from the *Sun* and four from the *Times*.

One experiment doesn't prove anything dispositively, but opinions in crossword land generally jibed with my conclusion that *Sun* and *Times* puzzles are of similarly high quality, and that they are indeed a notch or two above the rest of the crowd.

How should the *Times* proceed? They do have a simple solution to the *Sun*'s challenge, and it will be interesting to see if the paper values its crossword brand enough to implement it. By my estimate the *Times* earns several million dollars in profit annually off its crossword through syndication, book sales, charging solvers $34.95 per year for digital access to its puzzles, its 1-900 answers line, and other revenue streams. A source I consider reliable has indicated to me that the paper earns between $1 and $2 million per year on the 1-900 number alone, probably closer to the latter, and almost all of it pure profit.

If the *Times* were to take roughly $125,000 of those millions and raise the daily constructor rate from, say, $135 to $500, Shortz would get first crack at virtually every outstanding crossword puzzle in the country, and the *Times* puzzle would immediately become in actuality what everyone already thinks it is, the best crossword in the country by a wide margin. For the time being, and unless the *Sun* goes out of business, the reality will remain that, in terms of quality, the *Times* crossword is only the first among two equals.

This may suffice, and may be the route the *Times* management chooses, for it's cheaper, and it takes a long time for a crossword's reputation to fade even slightly (though perhaps less time in the Internet era than previously, since ideas and opinions can be shared so quickly now). Only time—and the *Times*—will tell. "I welcome the competition," Shortz told me in reference to Gordon, and the puzzle world is better for the battle.

I'm solving today's *New York Times* crossword. 7-down is four spaces long and I know the last two letters are both E's. The clue is "Support for a proposal." I stare at it for about twenty seconds before a smile breaks on my face: it's KNEE. As in, the knee that supports a man who's proposing marriage. I shake my head, the grin still there, and move on to the next clue.

That smile on my face is the end product: a human has been brought joy. I've outsmarted the Puzzlemaster, and I like it. True, it took me longer than it should have, but nobody needs to know that. The *New York Times* crossword is a terrific and important thing, and will remain so, and should.

CHAPTER 3

Books and Magazines

Sit & Solve books fly off the shelves—since their 2002 debut, they've consistently been one of the top-selling crossword book lines in the nation.

Why are they so successful? There is nothing particularly unusual about the puzzles in these little volumes—normal crosswords, well-written by well-known names in the field, a little on the small side at 10 x 10 squares each, but nothing really out of the ordinary.

What makes these little books big sellers is their distinctive packaging—each one is shaped like a toilet, and features a toilet seat on its front cover. The back cover gives you a look inside: just-flushed blue water swirls down into the bowl, accompanied by the words "Got a few minutes?"

Sit & Solve—get it? Not too high on the classy scale, but you can't argue with the market; these titles sell, and sell, and sell.

"They told me, 'Are you kidding? We're not publishing books with a toilet seat on the cover,' " laughs Peter Gordon of Sterling Publishing, describing the acquisition meetings where his supervisors repeatedly shot down his *Sit & Solve* idea. But after five years of pleading his case, Gordon says with a grin, "I finally wore them down. I mean, the toilet's where half the people are solving these things anyway."

The books took off right away, and are now a regular feature of the crossword puzzle section at your local bookstore. Go into any Barnes & Noble and you'll see them, dozens of crossword-filled crappers dangling from a specially-designed rack near the cash register. Customers snicker at the impudence—and snap them up as impulse buys in huge numbers.

Welcome to the contemporary crossword puzzle book market, where, as in other areas of commerce, the proverbial sizzle often matters more than the steak. And these days, as senior acquisitions editor at Sterling, Gordon is the master of crossword book sizzle (this is Gordon's day job; as we've already seen, he moonlights evenings as crossword editor for the *New York Sun*).

By dint of his position at Sterling, which is owned by Barnes & Noble, Gordon has final say on more original puzzle books than anyone else in the country. Crossword books fall into two broad categories, reprints and originals. Reprint books feature puzzles from the *New York Times*, *Washington Post*, *Los Angeles Times*, *Newsday*, and a few other papers, who simply reissue in book form the puzzles they've already published on newsprint. They might update the clues a bit if several years have passed since the original publication date, but they're essentially still the same puzzles.

The originals market consists of never-before-published puzzles, and has blossomed under Gordon's eight-year run at Sterling. The rise of big box booksellers has also ushered this new era along, since mega-stores like B&N and Borders can afford to hawk niche titles like *Baseball Crosswords* and *Classic Movie Crosswords* that their smaller predecessors just didn't have shelf space for. Amazon and online book-selling in general have likewise facilitated this growth.

Original books are gambles, and publishers tend to prefer the lower-risk, lower-cost approach of reprints. Puzzles in reprint books have already been paid for, so whatever the publisher sells is found money, as contributing constructors usually receive no royalties. Plus reprints already have a built-in audience, namely the readers of the newspaper whose puzzles are being reprinted. These reprint books indisputably sell well, especially the series of *New York Times* and *Newsday* puzzles, but the originals market is where all the fun and innovation is—and if a publishing house does it right, it can make a mint. "We'll try anything," Gordon says. "If it doesn't sell, then oh well—we'll just try something else."

I am on the Long Island Railroad on my way to Gordon's home in Great Neck, examining an extraordinary example of his "we'll try anything" crossword book publishing philos-ophy. It's a novelty book by Frank Longo given to me the evening before by Frank himself, who told me it had just been featured on the *Today* show as one of Gene Shalit's favorite new items of the year.

The World's Longest Crossword Puzzle, the book's title reads; the cover shows a thin ribbon of crossword grids stretching from planet Earth all the way into outer space. The crossword isn't *that* long, but it ain't short either:

twenty-one feet, ten inches according to the introduction, and a little more than two inches tall, according to my ruler. The pages unfold like an accordion between the two unattached covers of the book, so you could lay the whole thing out flat if you had enough room.

It may sound gimmicky, but I actually like Longo's book a whole bunch. Here's why: every couple of years I hear about some schmo trumpeting his "World's Largest Crossword!!!" to anyone who'll listen. Kitschy catalogs often carry something claiming that distinction, or gift stores, or game Web sites. But invariably, the puzzle doesn't live up to the hype: it fails to follow the standard conventions of crosswords, meaning that in order to get to "world's largest" size, the constructor had to cheat. He probably used two-letter words, an asymmetrical grid, repeat entries within the grid, or all of these, and who knows what other rules were broken along the way. On top of that, the clues are probably lousy, too, because the author isn't likely to be an actual crossword writer experienced in cluing.

Finally, these giga-crosswords are generally so physically awkward to solve that you'd probably get lumbago if you tried; the clue to a given entry might literally be four feet away from that entry's spot in the grid. Happy Birthday, Grandma—enjoy these hours and hours of lower back pain! I've seen it so often that all I can do when I hear about the latest "12 x 12 Foot Monster Crossword" is scoff and cluck and shake my round, jaded head.

But Frank's book is the real deal, avoiding these pitfalls with verve. Its grid is symmetrical, contains no two-letter words, and, amazingly, no repeated entries. That last part is mind-blowing since, as Longo points out in the introduction, the puzzle has 2,439 entries in total. That's roughly equivalent to thirty-three daily-size crosswords—and you'll never, ever solve thirty-three daily-size puzzles without hitting a whole passel of repeated grid entries.

And no chiropractor visits: the puzzle is laid out so the clues for a particular grid section are right beneath that grid section, which facilitates solving greatly. It's irrelevant, but I also appreciate the wryness of *The World's Longest Crossword Puzzle*'s author being named "Longo" (Gordon will tell me jokingly later, "That's pretty much why I picked Frank to write it").

One last clever touch: the further you progress in the puzzle, the tougher it gets. For instance, 1-down is a three-letter lob clued as "ChapStick target" (LIP, of course), but 2238-across (!) is the tricky "Event for the fleet" (RACE—"fleet" here meaning "quick").

Like I said: the originals market is where all the fun and innovation is.

I detrain and walk seven minutes to Gordon's suburban home, which he shares with his more-than-lovely wife (a dead ringer for Larry David's wife on *Curb Your Enthusiasm*), two adorable young daughters, and a constantly farting old bulldog ("Sorry about that," Gordon repeatedly pleads during my two-hour visit, striking match after match to mask the odor).

We head down the hallway to his small, extremely neat home office which contains all 300-plus puzzle books Gordon has shepherded through to publication during his eight years at Sterling. Some are normal puzzle book titles you'd expect, like *Celebrity Crosswords* or *10-Minute Crosswords*, while others are a little more offbeat, like *A to Z Crosswords*, in which every puzzle contains every letter of the alphabet at least one time. But back to the *Sit & Solves*.

"So these books started selling really well," Gordon tells me, "and then we thought: what if someone comes into the store and looks at these two"—he holds up two toilet-seat cover books, identical in appearance except for their different author bylines—"and they think, 'Hey, did I already buy that one? I don't remember.' So we thought, why not change the shape of the book? Why is it always a toilet seat?"

Keeping the name *Sit & Solve* but with a different take on the kind of sitting going on, Sterling launched a subline called *Sit & Solve Commuter Crosswords*, with books shaped like buses and trains and, in one instance, an everything bagel. A subline off that called *Sip & Solve* followed, for the same value of disambiguation, with covers featuring a coffee cup.

The packaging, then, is at least as important as the puzzles inside the book. "You can take a book that doesn't sell, reissue it with a new title, and it sells," Gordon explains. He would know: before his bosses agreed to publish the *Sit & Solve* toilet seat books, the first one had already appeared with a normal cover under the title *Mighty Mini Crosswords*. Reluctant to buy the toilet seat idea anyway, Barnes & Noble would not pay for new puzzles, but insisted instead that Gordon test the market by reissuing old puzzles, which he did.

And here's what happened: with the exact same crosswords in it, the first *Sit & Solve* crossword book with a toilet seat on the cover sold *eighteen times* as many copies as it had in its previous life as *Mighty Mini Crosswords*.

Title power doesn't just predominate with crossword books, either. When Sterling sought to cash in on the sudoku craze, Gordon's boss suggested they convey differing difficulty levels of their new line with titles like *Monday Sudoku* for the easiest, *Tuesday Sudoku* for the next, on up to *Friday Sudoku* for the toughest. When Gordon balked at the blandness of that, his boss hit back with the classic higher-up's rejoinder: fine, you come up with something better and have it on my desk ASAP.

That day, Gordon sketched out ideas, fully aware that the title of the series was going to be key in its success or failure. He felt certain the days of the week thing was too vanilla, but how else to communicate degrees of toughness to a potential book buyer as they scanned the shelves—and how to do it in a lively, novel way?

After a while, Gordon hit upon playing up the Japanese angle of sudoku. *Sushi Sudoku*? Kind of funny, but too ridiculous, and no obvious way to delineate difficulty. *Sumo Sudoku*? Not quite, but that at least makes more sense than *Sushi Sudoku*, since sumo is a competitive event with rankings.

How about karate? The idea began to gel: a series of books named for the belts given out in dojos. *White Belt Sudoku* for the easiest book, *Black Belt Sudoku* for the hardest, but what for the levels in between?

"And then I figured brown belt for the second hardest level, since everyone knows brown belt is the one right before black," Gordon explains, "and then something like green for the second easiest level," since even non-karate

fans would logically infer that green must be somewhere
between white and brown.

The books came out—*White Belt Sudoku, Green Belt
Sudoku, Brown Belt Sudoku,* and *Black Belt Sudoku*—and
became big sellers. The karate angle gave the books a cool
Japanese flavor, and the belt colors indicated quickly and
precisely to potential buyers what they were getting—and
did it in a neat way that you have to spend a couple of fun
seconds figuring out, which a book labeled *Easy Sudoku* or
Difficult Sudoku doesn't. When it was time for a second book
for each level, the titles were obvious: *Second Degree White
Belt Sudoku, Second Degree Black Belt Sudoku,* and so on.

So all the fun and innovation is in the originals market,
as I've stated. But perhaps that's a little too forcefully
phrased, since it turns out that there is indeed a bit of room
for ingenuity in the reprints market as well. Not so much in
the puzzles, since those are already set, but more in how
those puzzles are presented and sold. Just ask Stan
Newman, who is to the crossword reprints book market what
Peter Gordon is to the originals market: the main source of
innovation.

In 1999, Newman was part of a brainstorming session at
Random House, where he then worked as Puzzles and Games
Managing Director, when insight struck. In his trademark
Long Island accent Newman tells me, "I thought, what if we
put out a series of crossword books based not upon the specific content of the puzzles, or the level of difficulty, but on
the occasion on which people might buy a puzzle book. And
so we thought—on what occasion do people buy a crossword
book? Birthdays, Mother's Day, et cetera. In consultation

with sales and marketing people, we picked one—when they're going on vacation."

For a book of crosswords specifically sold to people getting away from it all, it was clear to Newman that they had to be fairly easy puzzles. So he packaged up a few dozen of the early-week crosswords from his syndicated *Newsday* puzzle, slapped the title *Vacation Crosswords* on the front, and then turned to the cover art.

"I didn't know exactly what I wanted," Newman says, "but I knew I wanted something that would convey a relaxing vacation."

The various decision-makers involved finally settled on a pair of beach chairs resting beneath an umbrella on a stretch of white, sandy beach. A seashell cradles the puzzle number on every page, and a crossword book aimed at vacationers was born.

The first *Vacation Crosswords* book appeared in 2000, and was "an immediate smash success," according to Newman. Evidently it was, since the formula was soon emulated by the *New York Times'* publisher, St. Martin's Press, which began putting out their own beachy crossword books of *Times* puzzle reprints that looked and felt suspiciously like the Random House books. Newman even prodded Random House to take legal action against St. Martin's for copyright infringement, but they chose not to.

(You be the judge: The original 2000 *Random House Vacation Crosswords, Volume 1* was subtitled "Breezy Crosswords Perfect for Relaxing" and featured on its cover a pair of beach chairs on the sand beneath an umbrella. The 2003 volume *The New York Times Crosswords for Your Beach Bag* is subtitled "75 Easy, Breezy Puzzles," and features on its cover a beach chair on the sand beneath an umbrella).

Other similar "occasion" titles followed, and all did well: *By the Fireside Crosswords, Cabin Fever Crosswords, Back to the Beach Crosswords, Fun in the Sun Crosswords,* and, inevitably, *More Vacation Crosswords.* All were just regular old *Newsday* reprints repackaged as tickets to tropical paradise or other similarly comfortable locales; in other words, pure sizzle.

Such ideas weren't actually new, it turned out, only so old that everyone had forgotten them. Newman possesses what he labels "The world's second-largest collection of puzzle books"—after Will Shortz's—and this gave him what he terms "historical perspective" on what the puzzle book-buying audience might want.

The "occasion" inspiration entered Newman's brain via an old book series he has from the 1940s. Published by Simon & Schuster, it was a line of puzzle books specifically for people recovering from an illness. They had intriguing, humorous titles like *Fun in Bed* and *Bedside Manna* (a puzzle book being manna for the bedridden). Such ideas had been forgotten in the intervening decades, as reliable reprints series like the *Times* came to dominate the market, along with the stalwart originals Simon & Schuster puzzle book series started by Margaret Farrar back in 1924 (which just hit Volume #250 in June of 2006). Newman had only to reinvent the wheel to add some zing to the reprints grind.

Bookswise, then, a crossword puzzle fan has many more options these days than he did a couple of decades ago, which is a good capitalist result. In the case of originals, the solver has a wider range of crossword styles and difficulty levels to choose from, plus a lot more fun novelty titles, which are also good things. The options available in the reprints market have perhaps not expanded quite so much, but the titles and cover art are snappier than they used to be, which, as it turns out, is roughly as important to the solver as the quality of the puzzles beneath that cover. I suppose I'm sneering a bit at that, but I do realize at least that my sneers are unjustified. I know little about wine, after all, but when I do buy a bottle, I judge the content based on the label. I have no other way to differentiate between vintage and plonk, and might lack the palate to tell from a sip or two anyway.

When she still ran the company, Penny Kanter liked to draw a triangle to illustrate her target market. At the top point of the triangle were elite puzzle solvers—people who could blaze through a *New York Times* Monday puzzle in five minutes flat and polish off a Saturday in under fifteen. Impressive feats, but Kanter wasn't really interested in these people, since there are relatively few of them out there.

The nearer you got to its base, the wider the triangle got. This was her market, the fat part of the puzzle-solving curve, and it's still the main market of the puzzle magazine company that bears her name, Penny Press. Most of Penny Press's target solvers couldn't knock off a Saturday *Times* puzzle in three hours, much less fifteen minutes, but they enjoy a fun solve nonetheless, and Penny Press gives it to them. These puzzles are the Budweiser of crosswords—not the top of the line, but reliable and inexpensive and unpretentious and pretty good, and sometimes just the thing you need. Unlike Bud, though, Penny Press aims at elderly, female Middle America instead of middle-aged, male Middle America.

"We tried for a high-end magazine with *Joy of Crosswords*, but it didn't work," says Tom Schaumann, the goateed managing editor at Penny Press. That magazine eventually got yanked from the rotation, since people who want elite-level crosswords just don't think of the Penny Press name. Instead they go for *New York Times* puzzle books or a small handful of high-level magazines like *Crosswords Crosswords* or *GAMES World of Puzzles*. But don't feel bad for Penny Press, since, as Schaumann tells me, "These lower-difficulty puzzles fly off the shelves." Indeed they must, since Penny Press is the largest puzzle magazine company in the country.

I visit Penny Press's offices in the charming maritime city of Norwalk, Connecticut, on a sunny spring day in the low sixties. Their site is a three-story office building situated incongruously in a residential neighborhood with a resort feel to it; lime green and canary yellow houses populate 150-yard-long Prowitt Street, and you can almost smell the sea air, since we're six blocks from the water. I'm a half hour early so I make the ten-minute jaunt to Norwalk's harbor before heading back to Penny Press, passing stores like Fisherman's World Complete Tackle Center and signs advertising the Maritime Aquarium. Dry-docked boat hulls dominate the horizon down by the shore.

Penny Press takes up all three floors of the building, and regular *New York Times* crossword constructor Eric Berlin gives me the grand tour. The bearded, bespectacled thirty-eight-year-old works days in Penny Press's business office, tracking which of the company's eighty-odd puzzle magazines are doing well, which aren't doing well, what new titles they ought to put out, and what titles need to be axed. As Berlin himself describes his job: "I ask myself: is this title trending down? Why is it trending down? And what can we do about it?"

The top floor is the editorial department, a few dozen mostly-female employees scattered throughout a warren of cubicles, fact-checking and test-solving a huge variety of puzzles sent in by freelance constructors from around the country. Here Berlin introduces me to David Lindsey, a dapper, elderly, bowtie-sporting gentleman lunching at his desk while editing a Crushword puzzle (a crossword where a single square can have several letters written in it).

"I have been at Penny Press for over twenty years," Lindsey intones when I ask, then mentions that he even worked a stint at Penny Press's long-defunct parent company in the 1960s. "I specialize in variety puzzles," he adds, which explains his utility and longevity; in addition to crosswords, Penny Press magazines contain over 500 other types of variety puzzles, like cryptic crosswords, anagrams, and Lindsey's personal favorite, a hybrid head-scratcher called the "Chess-word Puzzle."

Further around the cubicle circuit we pass a rainbow wall of enormous puzzle books. "I don't even know what these are," Berlin exclaims ("Penny Press Art Department," I hear a guy nearby answering his phone). They're enormous volumes of magazine crosswords reprinted in book form, it turns out, though where and how they're sold isn't clear to either of us, and Berlin is one of the company's key employees; this is a vast operation. Next to these big books lie shelves of "generics," thin, single-puzzle volumes sold only by mail, not in bookstores. House ads in the magazines let solvers who are fans of a particular kind of variety puzzle order books of that puzzle only. "People get hooked on one kind of puzzle, and they order generics," Berlin says.

Next we come upon a shrinelike cave of books with a single table in the middle, lit dimly by one overheard fluorescent bulb. "The reference library," Berlin proclaims. This small room of perhaps 2,000 volumes includes a slew of dictionaries, half a shelf of Leonard Maltin movie guides from years past, and another half shelf of books devoted to matters floral with titles like *An Instant Guide to Trees* and *What's New in Gardening*. Useful for looking up plant-related clues, I imagine.

Berlin and I head down to the second floor, where we pass the giant crossword grid backdrop behind the company's main reception area. This floor is the business side of the publication, where financial and personnel decisions are made; Berlin's own cube is here. "This is where we deal with distributors, and getting the magazines into newsstands and supermarkets and 7-11's," he says.

The first floor is the company's fulfillment and customer service center, where subscriber payments are processed. Here I find Chris Roy, a young man whose job it is to handle subscription cards as they come in.

"They can either check 'payment included,' or 'bill me later,'" Roy explains, holding up the filled-out subscription card of a woman named Carol whose address is in Iowa. Roy handles the payment accordingly based on whether the subscriber has sent the check along with the card or elects to be billed later. In the cubicles around Roy I hear the computers of his colleagues, again mostly women, clicking away at this and the myriad other mundane but necessary clerical tasks involved in running several dozen puzzle magazines.

Over lunch at a harborside seafood restaurant in Norwalk, Chris Begley lets me in on some of the secrets of the puzzle magazine business. Begley is a fortyish woman with long, light-brown hair and a big smile, and associate publisher at Penny Press. She's also married to Schaumann; they have three kids together, and in fact met at Penny Press sixteen years ago. "You're a puzzling power couple," I tell Begley, who flashes her grin and replies, "Yeah, I guess you might say that."

But on to business: "We survey our customers," Begley tells me, "and they say, 'I only buy Penny Press' or 'I only buy Dell' and 'I'll go to a different store if they don't have my favorite title.'" So brand loyalty is strong among puzzle solvers; indeed, when Penny Press acquired Dell's puzzle magazines in 1996, they didn't dare tinker with the Dell name or any of their popular magazine titles.

Along with us at the lunch is Berlin, who assists Begley in keeping an overall vision of the Penny Press magazine mix. It's an inexact science: "In some cases there's no difference in content or difficulty," Begley says, but one title may flourish and the other need to be cut. Last year, for instance, a variety puzzle magazine called *Fast 'N' Fun Fill-Ins* got pulled from the lineup due to weak sales. It had been strong for years, but then began to slump, and was finally whacked. Other similar titles, like *Favorite Fill-Ins* and *Penny's Famous Fill-Ins*, remained strong during the *Fast 'N' Fun Fill-Ins* decline. "Why one title's doing well and others aren't is often a mystery to me," Berlin laments, "but there's no denying the numbers. The masses have spoken."

"Odie Approved!" reads the cover of *Garfield Word Seeks* magazine, which I take out and place on our lunch table; right beside those two words Garfield's canine buddy gives the solver a thumbs-up sign. The famed fat orange cat himself is front and center on the purple cover, solving a word find that includes the entries "lasagna," "catnap," and "lazy."

It may sound like an odd match, but *Garfield Word Seeks* is one of Penny Press's top sellers. It moves so well, in fact, that the company recently increased the frequency of the title from six times a year to nine. As with the crossword book market—and the wine market, and the beer market—such cover branding is nearly as important as the quality of what's inside.

Begley explains that branding the puzzles with well-known names like Garfield is just a way of differentiating certain titles from the rest of the crowd. Not every idea succeeds: a NASCAR-themed puzzle magazine was pulled after five issues due to weak sales, for instance, but their Nickelodeon-branded magazine of kids' puzzles sells well. Begley and Berlin also have high hopes for a new celebrity-branded variety title, "Pat Sajak's Get-A-Letter Crosswords," which uses a gimmick that Sajak himself purportedly came up with: certain squares within a standard crossword contain a symbol, like a star or a heart. Each square with a given symbol will always wind up containing the same letter; all the stars in a puzzle might be L's, for instance, or all the hearts G's, so once a solver figures out one heart-square, she's got all the heart-squares nailed. It's a cute, novel solving aid, and Sajak's name (and face) on the cover won't hurt sales a bit.

Penny Press naturally didn't miss the sudoku wave, either. "Sudoku was something we could introduce quickly because the puzzles are computer-generated," Begley tells me. In April of 2005 the staff was already discussing the idea, and by September, they had their first title on the shelves ("I spent my summer vacation last year test-solving sudoku-generating programs," Tom Schaumann had told me earlier in the day).

Price is also key in the puzzle magazine market. "A lot of the people who buy our magazines are on fixed incomes, so they're sensitive to price," Begley says. Some of Penny Press's 80-page titles sell for as little as 99 cents, while the solver who spashes out for a $7.99 volume gets a gargantuan 272-page puzzle tome.

When I say, "So customers would notice the difference in price between a $2.99 title and a $4.99 title," Berlin practically jumps out of his chair. "My God, yes," he sputters. "Even a 50-cent difference in price is huge."

"Would they notice the difference between $2.95 and $2.99?" I reply, intending it as a joke.

"Well, no, probably not," Berlin concedes, but only after thinking about it for a moment.

• • •

There are really only two puzzle magazine companies in the country, Penny Press and Kappa Publishing, which operates out of a suburb of Philadelphia. Kappa is the publisher of *GAMES Magazine* and its offshoots, plus many other puzzle titles. The two companies together publish about 98 percent of the puzzle magazines in the country, "although it may be more than that," Berlin tells me. "I always give people the 98 percent figure, but I don't even know who that other 2 percent is, or if they really even exist." For all intents and purposes, if you buy a puzzle magazine in the U.S., it comes from either Penny Press or Kappa.

As you might expect, they keep tabs on each other pretty closely. Many of their titles are almost indistinguishable: Kappa's include *Collector's Crosswords, Superb Crosswords, Easy Crosswords,* and *Simple Crosswords,* while Penny Press's titles include *Take-A-Break Easy Crosswords, Good Time Crossword Puzzles, Easy Crossword Express,* and *Fast & Easy Crosswords.*

"We do everything from easier than *TV Guide* to harder than the *New York Times*," Judy Weightman of Kappa tells me when I run into her at the American Crossword Puzzle Tournament. They put out around twenty-five different crossword magazines, plus logic titles, cryptogram titles, and, of course, six or eight sudoku titles.

Virtually all of the easy-and medium-level crosswords in puzzle magazines these days are computer-generated; the high-end stuff is still written by humans. Both companies have done a good job of reducing the amount of cross-wordese in their puzzles, but it's been a decades-long process: "I've spent more of my life than I care to think about removing Bulgarian coins and Cambodian rivers from grids," Weightman says.

It's been years since I've done so, but on the train back from Norwalk I decide to solve a couple of easy and medium crosswords from a Penny Press magazine, *Dell Crossword & Variety Special.* I grew up solving Penny Press and Dell puzzles, and a math game called cross sums was always one of my favorites. Cross sums is set for bigger and better things these days, having recently been given the Japanese name *kakuro* and publicized as the next post-sudoku wave of Japanese puzzle craze. I spot a cross sums in the magazine and smile; for me, leafing through this is a pleasant trip down Memory Lane.

I open to the first crossword in the book, labeled EASY, which it is. I'm able to guess about 90 percent of the words right when I read the clue for the first time: "At the head of the line" is FIRST, "Nervous twitch" is TIC, and "School of higher education" is COLLEGE. There is no theme to the puzzle, and there aren't any clues I'd label as clever in the entire thing, but that's fine: this is supposed to be an easy, straightforward crossword, and that's what it is. To the puzzle's credit, there is no crosswordese at all in it, every single grid entry being something an adult with a high school education would know.

Beneath this crossword is a quick variety puzzle I find modestly charming. It's a list of supposed bestselling books you have to match up with a second list of their supposed authors. *Shopping on Credit* the adept solver will match with the name "U. Ken Bilmy," while *Secrets of Successful Families* was penned by a woman with the unlikely name of "Charity B. Ginzatt-Holm."

Cute in a corny way, but I'm here to survey the crosswords, so I move on to a medium. As advertised, the words indeed get a shade tougher: TAM ("Scottish cap") makes an appearance, as does ENS ("Type widths"). The puzzle has an old-fashioned feel to it, since the framework for the pop culture referenced is centered around the middle of the 20th-century: IVES is "Burl of film," ELLA is "Ms. Fitzgerald," ELI is "Actor Wallach," and YUL is "Mr. Brynner." It wouldn't be my personal choice, but it's perfect for the demographic of most puzzle magazines: women over the age of sixty. "Most of our subscribers are women, maybe around 95 percent, and they tend to be senior citizens," Berlin says. They don't want Norah Jones and Charlize Theron in their puzzles, because they don't know who those people are and they don't care. They want Burl Ives and Ella Fitzgerald (and Ava Gardner and Eve Arden), so that's what Penny Press gives them, at least in the easier puzzles; in the magazine's tougher crosswords I notice a few more modern references, like ANI clued as "Singer DiFranco," and even "Internet annoyances" for POP-UP MESSAGES.

According to Will Shortz, the first crossword puzzle magazine was called *Fad*, and published in New York City in January 1925. "While nominally covering all fads and hobbies," Shortz writes me in an e-mail, "*Fad*'s first two issues are devoted almost entirely to crosswords, making this the first known crossword magazine in the world."

We've come a long way in the intervening eight decades. Though crossword magazines nowadays tend to serve puzzle solvers who aren't looking for a brain-crushing challenge, but rather a pleasurable, somewhat easy solve, there's no reason such puzzles can't be fresh and enjoyable. The two companies that provide almost the entirety of the country's puzzle magazines do that well. In combination with the expanding crossword book market, today's crossword solver suffers an embarrassment of choice. Since puzzles are entertainment, this is as it ought to be. I suspect the editors of *Fad* would be proud of what they started.

CHAPTER 4

Glad and Grateful

About fifteen people in the United States earn their living primarily from writing crossword puzzles.

True, another several dozen are crossword editors at newspapers or magazines, and a further couple hundred write them as a hobby, a way to fill the retirement years, or a modest supplemental income to a normal day job. But if you're looking for people who wake up 230 mornings a year and write crosswords most of the day and pay their bills with the scant dough those puzzles bring in, there's really just fifteen of them. Or of "us," I should say, because I'm a member of that little group.

Moneywise, this isn't the easiest thing to pull off. I've already whined that the *New York Times* gives constructors just $135 for a daily puzzle, and that's pretty much the high end of the payment scale. Besides, most markets pay not when they accept your crossword, but only when it actually gets published, which will be months (if you're lucky) or years (if you're not) after it's been submitted. Even then, you'll sometimes need to shoot your overworked editor an e-mail or two to nudge that money along—and don't forget to send the taxman his slice of your little pie. Bizet called music a fine art but a sad profession. The same might be said of crossword puzzle writing, but financially, it's sadder than merely sad. It's downright comical.

You can't complain about starving artisthood, but artists still do. Grandmasters complain they can't scratch a living from chess because most people would rather play video games. Poets complain they can't make ends meet since people would rather read King than Browning, if they read anything at all. But neither has a whine worth listening to, since the grandmaster doesn't buy volumes of verse and the poet doesn't fork money over to watch chess tournaments. Each artist decries society at large for failing to appreciate him, but each is also a member of the other's decried society.

So no, shaking your fist at the universe doesn't get you anywhere. But there is something the minor artist can do to find his place in the sun: he can hustle. He can self-pimp. He can push the product. Yes it's a lot of work, yes you'll have to learn money to earn money, yes your art will get lost in the process, and even if you do succeed—and you probably won't—you may wind up wondering if you've really succeeded at all.

Oh, and it's demeaning, too: I once paid my rent by writing a tabbies-themed crossword puzzle for a cat magazine. The clue for 18-across was "It might flatten when tabby's angry" and the answer was EAR. Not quite Michelangelo at the Sistine Chapel, but the check cleared, and I could always hope that time would bring better things.

The first crossword puzzle I ever submitted for publication

was a so-called "rebus theme." It was 1986, I was a thirteen-year-old crossword fan growing up in the Maryland suburbs, and rebus themes were still cool. The puzzle was rejected anyway.

The cover letter couldn't have helped, since it was a stylistic monstrosity. Addressed to Wayne Robert Williams, editor of the once great but now defunct *Dell Champion Crossword Puzzles*, it radiated unprofessionalism since I'd typed it on college-rule paper. Picture the blue lines of rule ink bisecting entire lines of poorly-spaced text; not the way to make an impression on an editor.

But the rebus theme should have saved it. In the 1950s constructor Bernice Gordon injected new life into crosswords with a novel idea. Tired of being bound to the concept that each square in a puzzle had to be filled with a letter, she foisted a trick on solvers: in each of the theme entries in her puzzle, one square would need to be filled not with a letter, but with a *symbol*. In Gordon's puzzle that symbol was an ampersand, and stood not necessarily for the word "and," but for the letters AND. So the nine-letter answer to the clue "Much of Northern Europe" wasn't SCANDINAVIA, which wouldn't fit, but SC&INAVIA. The answer to "Singer with a fruit basket" was only eleven letters long, all you needed for the normally thirteen-letter-long name CARMEN MIR&A.

Rebus puzzles are a tad passé these days, since every plausible keyword, like AND above, has been used many times over, and even the stretches have been given more than one shot. But this was the mid-1980s, and rebus puzzles hadn't yet worn out their welcome, so I decided to make solvers look for KEYs in the puzzle: in certain squares, they'd have to draw in a little key to complete that answer.

One of the finer points of constructing rebus puzzles is to divide the letters in the keyword in different ways. This is seen as both more challenging for the solver and more elegant from a constructing point of view. For instance, if a constructor chose (as zillions have) to make a rebus puzzle with the keyword STAR, he could easily fill a grid with theme words like BATTLE* GALACTICA, *LIGHT EXPRESS, DON'T *T WITH ME, and so on.

Far more elegant, however, would be to split the keyword in various ways, such as CO*ICA for "Neighbor of Nicaragua" or "TWI*OUND" for "Distort the meaning of, as someone's words."

The "keys" puzzle featured such splits: in addition to the non-split (KEY)HOLES and PASS(KEY) and ANKARA, TUR(KEY), the puzzle contained both PIN(K EY)E ("Ocular trouble") and MA(KE Y)OU (clued as "I'm gonna ___ an offer you can't refuse").

Williams wound up rejecting the puzzle, primarily because the MA(KE Y)OU entry is a "partial," or part of a quote, which is acceptable for a normal answer but considered highly inelegant for a theme answer. He was kind enough to a write a detailed, one-and-a-half page critique of both the puzzle and the cover letter, explaining patiently where I'd gone wrong. He suggested, for instance, that a revision of this theme idea might include a full phrase such as "I LI(KE Y)OUR STYLE" instead of the awkward partial "MA(KE Y)OU."

Quickly thereafter, I sent two more submissions to Williams at *Dell Champion Crossword Puzzles*. He accepted

both and in November of 1986 they became my first published crosswords. My mom and I bought six copies of the
magazine at the local Peoples Drugstore—now, like *Dell
Champion*, no longer with us—where my hands trembled as
I located the magazine on the rack, opened it, and saw the
words "by Matthew Gaffney." Cool!

Every teenager finds his or her mother embarrassing at
times, but mine was especially so on that particular day. At
the checkout counter, she for some reason had to tell the
attractive, roughly eighteen-year-old cashier, "He wrote two
crossword puzzles in here!" and then actually opened the
magazine up and showed them to her. Naturally the hottie
cashier couldn't have cared less, and it'd be difficult to
choreograph a more embarrassing teenage moment (or one
involving crossword puzzles, at least).

One of those two debut puzzles had both an unspeakably
lame title ("TV Classics") and an unspeakably lame theme
(the only two theme entries in the grid were ALFRED
HITCHCOCK and THE TWILIGHT ZONE). But the other
one, another rebus theme, was pretty good—and would have
been great, in fact, if not for a stumble.

The keyword was USA (for which the solver could draw a
little map of the U.S. in the relevant boxes, or simply
squeeze the letters USA into them), and the four theme
entries split the keyword nicely: SAY YO(U, SA)Y ME
("*White Nights* song"), MARC(US A)LLEN ("1981 Heisman
winner"), (USA) FOR AFRICA ("'We Are the World'
recorders"), and SEEKING S(USA)N ("*Desperately* ___
(Madonna movie)").

Even twenty years later, though, when I look back on this

last theme entry, I cringe at its inelegance. The puzzle was close to being a model rebus theme, since each of the four theme entries used the keyword in a different way (U/SA, US/A, USA as a word, and USA hidden in a larger word). But SEEKING SUSAN is a blot, since like, MAKE YOU in the KEY puzzle, it's a partial quote, and therefore pretty gross as a theme entry. Williams let this go because the rest of the puzzle was good, but why couldn't I find a SUSAN with a seven-letter surname, which would've made the theme perfect? I recall trying, but it was surprisingly tough—Susan ANTHONY is really "Susan B. Anthony," Susan ESTRICH wasn't yet famous, and actress Susan ST. JAMES actually spells her surname "Saint James"—but I wish I'd been able to come up with something else besides the partial.

These two puzzles were published a week shy of my fourteenth birthday. A month later, I received a check from Dell for $80, which my dad paid me cash for and had me sign over to him, since I didn't have a bank account of my own at the time.

Ten years later, while looking through the "kids' file" he'd kept on my sister, brother, and me, I found the check, still pristine.

"You never cashed this?" I asked him.

"Of course not," he said. "I'd never do that."

But I talked him into it, since $80 is $80. I contacted Dell, who reissued the check, fully a decade later, and bought groceries with the paternally-financed double payment.

Shortly after those two puzzles appeared, I received a letter from a person who introduced himself as Stan Newman. He said he'd seen my puzzles in *Dell Champion* and wanted to know if I'd be interested in doing one for a publication he edited, *The Crossworder's OWN Newsletter*. It was the newsletter's habit of running a small bio of constructors making their debut in the publication, so he also asked for a few words about myself in addition to the puzzle.

I sent Stan a 15 x 15 entitled "Three Times Fives," where the three theme entries—GREAT WHITE SHARK, CHRIS EVERT LLOYD, and NOBEL PEACE PRIZE—were three-word phrases comprised only of five-letter words (the title itself is another example of the theme, in fact). My bio in the newsletter noted that my "hobbies include bowling, Latin, and chess." It was my third published crossword, and I really liked having that Z in the theme entry (NOBEL PEACE PRIZE). When I started solving crosswords at about age nine, I realized that constructors who really knew what they were doing could work a lot of the four rarest letters (Q, Z, X, and J) into their grids. Anyone can make a grid full of E's and N's and S's and T's, and of course even the best cruciverbalists need to use these letters in their puzzles. But I made a habit at that time of counting up the number of those four rarest letters in a puzzle after I'd solved it. I frowned upon the puzzles with zero; one or two at least showed some effort; but the people who could stuff six or eight or even ten of that lofty quartet into a 15 x 15 grid—that I really admired, and tried to emulate, and still do. Last year I finished a book for an editor, who called me up and said, "You sure have a lot of X's and J's and Z's and Q's in here." I glowed with pride for the rest of the day.

I also realized early on that especially skilled constructors could include wide-open patterns with few black squares
in their grids. As with the rare letters, anyone can fill a grid
with lots of compartmentalized little 3 x 4 areas demarcated
by tons of black squares, but the pros could weave grids with
huge fields of white—and even sneak a couple of X's and Z's
into those fields. It was the difference between dumping in a
perfunctory lay-up in practice and swishing a thirty-footer
with a defenseman in your face during a game; I came to
greatly admire those who could do it (the six I found most
awe-inspiring comprise this book's dedicatees). I didn't just
admire their style; I wanted to be a part of it.

Throughout my high school years, I continued to publish
more crosswords in *Dell Champion* and then branched out to
other markets, including *Newsday* and some specialty pub-
lications like *The Crosswords Club* and *The Uptown Puzzle
Club*. My GPA drifted ever southward as I clandestinely
composed crossword grids on sheets of graph paper hidden
under (and often, in) Latin and chemistry textbooks. There
was one 15 x 15 grid by Merl Reagle I became so enamored
with that I must've written it out from memory a hundred
times during especially dull classroom lectures. To this day
I can still recall the entire grid with ease—and occasionally
write it out in full, just to prove I can still do it.

My teachers didn't seem to get my hobby, though. In tenth
grade English class we had to give an informative speech on
any topic we chose, so I whipped up a crossword with every
member of the class's surname in it and talked for eight minutes about matters cruciverbal.

I even started the presentation off with a bang, which Mr. Simmons had told us was key in order to grab the audience's attention. "It's a six-letter word starting with G-E-N," I began, "and the clue is 'Sex.'" A few of the girls giggled and Mr. Simmons, a well-churched Oklahoman, shot me a stern look that said, "Where are you going with this?"

"Your mind races through the possibilities," I continued, "until you finally realize, after a few moments of thought, that the answer . . . is . . . *gender.*"

And I only got a B! Not fair at all. Simmons' only negative comment was "Why not tell us how to make our own crossword puzzle?" He was a tough grader, but I really believe he didn't give me the A because of the sex clue introduction.

I also showed Mrs. Heyman my crosswords in *Dell Champion*, and I figured, as an English teacher, she'd appreciate it. Nice lady and great teacher, but she barely reacted. "Too bad you can't apply this energy to your class work," she said. And she was right—I'd been lousy about keeping up with our reading of the *Odyssey*—but still, I realized I wasn't going to get much official teacher encouragement for my extracurricular crossword activities.

After gathering enough clips during my high school years, I decided in 1990 that I was ready to go for it. I was going to submit a crossword to the *New York Times*.

In 1990, I sent Eugene T. Maleska a note expressing interest in contributing puzzles to his paper. I didn't know at the time about his reputation for prickliness, so the letter I got back surprised me.

Maleska curtly explained that he didn't publish new constructors (I had been publishing puzzles for four years at
that point, and said as much in my note to him) and that, if
I could get three puzzles published elsewhere and send
them to him, he "might consider opening the gates." In
those years the *Times* paid only $175 for a Sunday crossword
and $50 for a daily puzzle, which was lower than most other
markets anyway, and you didn't have to put up with this
"opening the gates" crap (I found out later that Maleska
made a habit of not knowing—or pretending not to know—
who other people in the crossword world were).

I wasn't exactly a crossword superstar, but I had published
enough that Maleska should probably have known my name;
but even if he hadn't, there was no need to actively dis-
courage potential constructors. I found his letter annoying,
but my reaction was simply what Liz Gorski's reaction had
been when Maleska sent her a nasty note: I never sent him
any puzzles. Multiply that reaction times several dozen top
crossword constructors, and you get a lesser product.

Over the next few years I expanded my freelance clips to
the *Washington Post Magazine* (which brought a little local
celebrity, since I was in the D.C. area. I recall hearing the
delivery guy tossing the paper onto our driveway from his
car, running out at dawn, and tearing open the huge Sunday
Post to see my debut puzzle there in 1992), Simon and
Schuster's crossword book series, and *Random House Mas-
terpiece Crosswords,* another of Stan Newman's projects for
which he asked sixteen top puzzlewriters to construct three
crosswords each for an elegant, hardbound book.

Despite all these credits, I still hadn't been in the *Times,* and that irritated me, since non-crossword people kept asking why. No matter how much I explained to them that the *Times* wasn't really the best around, that didn't jibe with the conventional wisdom they knew, so it just wound up leaving most people confused.

Maleska died in 1993 and Will Shortz took over. I'd met Shortz in person at a crossword tournament a few years prior, so when the *Times* took him on board, I immediately sent him a Sunday-size crossword called "Famous Dieters." The theme's trick was to remove foods from famous people's names. For example, "Former Canadian prime minister" was not PIERRE TRUDEAU, but, RRE TRUDEAU (take his PIE away, and he's on a diet). "Former Supreme Court justice" wasn't OLIVER WENDELL HOLMES but O WEN-DELL HOLMES, after removing LIVER (that's a tricky one, since, oddly enough, either the first or last letter of Holmes' first name can be removed to leave a five-letter food).

Shortz's response was in sharp contrast to Maleska's: "I'm happy to publish your 'Dieters' puzzle," he wrote me, "since it's a handsome construction with a lot of lively vocabulary."

Was that so tough? You be a little nice to people, and they want to work with you. And it was no fluke. With his kind demeanor and superior editing style, Shortz brought back into the *Times* fold a slew of constructors who'd been turned off by Maleska.

The "Famous Dieters" puzzle was published in July of 1994. Over the rest of the '90s I published fifty-seven more puzzles with Shortz in the *Times,* an era during which it reclaimed its role as the best daily crossword in the land. I was glad to be a small part of it.

● ● ●

Still, it wasn't a living. Good conversation starter at parties, yes; reliable source of income, no way. One of the innovations Will Shortz brought to the *Times* puzzles was to increase the amount of pay constructors get, logically reasoning that it would lead to higher-quality submissions. When he took over, pay increased for daily puzzles (from $50 to $75) and for Sunday puzzles, which are much larger than dailies (from $150 to $300).

These figures blow the minds of most people who hear them, especially those in the media who are familiar with rates for freelance writers. A high quality *Times* crossword puzzle, which will literally be enjoyed by millions of people, can take anywhere from four to twelve hours to construct. For that effort, the constructor—and there are only a couple hundred people who can really make a *Times*-quality, top-level puzzle—would get just enough money to make a halfway decent grocery run, if he clipped coupons.

And that was the high end of the pay scale. The structure at the *Times* is similar to other freelance crossword markets: the editors receive good salaries, but the freelancers who actually make the puzzles get only a small amount, since it's a buyer's market. There are simply more people who want to publish a crossword in the *New York Times*, and who can make a decent-enough crossword, than there are spaces for those puzzles.

Again to use the *Times* as an example: they publish 365 crosswords per year. In a given year, they typically print the work of about 110 different constructors. Some are one-hit wonders, some are skilled hobbyists who are happy to toss in a puzzle every few months, and a few are the regulars. My high year at the *Times* was 1997, when I had fourteen crosswords published there; not bad, but the leader that year was ironman Rich Norris with twenty-two.

But do the depressing math: even if you were Rich Norris, and say five of your 22 puzzles were Sunday-sized, you're still only looking at $(5 \times \$300) + (12 \times \$75) = \$2,775$ for the whole year (minus Uncle Sam's cut). Some lower-paying gigs need more puzzles than the *Times*, but the higher number of puzzles is, of course, offset by the lower pay.

The *Times* will run a constructor's puzzle in their paper, syndicate it out to hundreds of other papers, reprint it in book form (often several times), and feature it online at their subscription-based site, but the constructor receives no royalties on any of this. You don't even get a free copy of the book your puzzle's reprinted in.

The upshot is that it's damn hard to make a living at freelance crossword puzzle writing; in fact, it's more or less impossible. I know because I wound up trying it, and failed.

Prior to January 1995, I'd called myself a "semiprofessional cruciverbalist." I always had other jobs: clerk in a video store, summer camp counselor, chess teacher. But as my early twenties became my mid-twenties, none of these jobs looked like a career. So I took the plunge: I would do what I was put on this Earth to do, and I would do it for a living. I would write crossword puzzles professionally.

That was the plan, anyway.

I was living in a group house in Frostburg, Maryland, a placid little college town in the low mountains of the state's western panhandle. I had a lot of friends who went to school in town, so my social life was more active than my bank account.

In addition to the low pay described above and the interminable waits for checks to arrive, there is another daunting obstacle awaiting the aspiring freelance crossword puzzle constructor: rejection rate. Will Shortz receives around seventy-five puzzles each week, and can only use seven. Not all of those seventy-five are publication-worthy, of course, but most are, and many very good pieces of work have to be rejected simply because they don't have a certain zip that pushes them over the threshold ("It just didn't grab me" is a standard phrase Shortz uses in rejection notes for puzzles like this). So Shortz has to pass on around 90 percent of the puzzles sent to him. Lesser markets have higher rates of acceptance, but correspondingly lower pay.

This meant that after laboriously printing the puzzle out, packing it up, sending it off, and waiting for a reply, there was a decent chance that it wouldn't even be accepted. Then I'd have to print it out again, pack it up again, and send it off to a lower-paying market, hoping this time for a yes (and I did indeed have to go through the trouble of reprinting and repackaging a rejected puzzle before sending it out again, since it's a turn off to an editor if dog-eared pages betray that they're getting another editor's leftovers).

I began to grow bitter about things during this period. I was producing what I felt were excellent crossword puzzles, enjoyed by hundreds of thousands or even millions of people, but was receiving only a pittance for them, and having to wait eons even to receive that. Plus, I was completely at the mercy of editors. In one case, a major crossword publication announced that it would start paying only $45 per crossword when it had previously paid $60, and this change was to take place retroactively, on crosswords they had already accepted for publication. Unlike prose writers, crossword writers are mostly hobbyists and therefore un-unionized, which leaves them powerless in situations like this. Overnight, the puzzles of mine that had been accepted for publication by this magazine sank in value from around $3,600 to around $2,700.

I complained, and eventually they agreed to pay me the previously agreed upon sum, but as the checks trickled in over the months and years, about half were for $60, the other half for $45. Every time it happened I'd have to call or e-mail to complain, and it was such a small amount to be haggling over. The life of a starving artist is indeed romantic, but only to those who aren't actually living it. The truth is, it's just plain dreary.

There had been one bright spot during this financially grim period. One day in early 1997, the following notice appeared on cruciverb-L, an online Web site where crossword constructing geeks hang out and exchange info:

> Hi there. Q Syndicate is looking for a constructor for 15 x 15 Jewish-themed crosswords, of the standard symmetrical type (not merely skeletal). Jewish themes and as much Jewish material as possible in the filler clues. Constructors will be paid. Inquiries: xxxxxx@aol.com or call 1-888-383-xxxx. Thanks for your time. Dave Bianco

I'm not Jewish, but my first girlfriend was. We were ten, she was a foot taller than me, our relationship lasted eighteen hours, and I cried when she ended it. I got over that setback eventually (by the following morning, in fact— young people are tough) and, having grown up with many Jewish friends, figured I could fake it for this gig. I told the editor I wasn't Jewish, but he never mentioned it to the papers he syndicated the puzzle to; it aided our charade that my Irish surname happens to have a Jewish twin.

I answered the ad, made a sample puzzle, and got the job. Over the next three years, for fifty bucks a pop, I made one Jewish-themed crossword puzzle per week, which Bianco syndicated out to Jewish newspapers across the country.

This experience taught me three valuable lessons. First, it was great to get those regular monthly checks of $200 or $250. None of this waiting seasons or years to get paid; it showed me that the crossword puzzle standard of being paid seasons or years after submittal was not necessarily normal.

Second, I learned computers. Unlike most crossword editors at the time, Bianco was highly computer literate, and insisted I learn the ins and outs of making and sending crosswords over e-mail. I downloaded this graphics program and that crossword exporting program until my trusty Hewlett-Packard had all the software gadgets a professional crossword constructor needed.

At that time, many crossword editors were still using Gutenberg-era, non-computerized technology. You'd construct your puzzle on graph paper (seems comical now, but that's how we did it), type the clues up on a word processor or a typewriter, transfer the grid by hand to a larger grid (including writing all the little numbers in the squares, and cross-hatching the black squares in), and snail mail it off to the editor with an SASE, which you got back weeks or months later with an acceptance note or rejection letter.

The Internet revolution had just started to hit crossword puzzles around then, but I hadn't jumped on the bandwagon yet, since I hadn't had to: many editors were along in years, and hoping to never have to really learn computers. With "Puzzle Tov," as we named the feature, I had to learn the cyberstuff.

Third, and very importantly for my later work, I learned to clue to the customer. The idea behind Puzzle Tov was to have as many of the clues and answers be as Jewish as possible. With some words, this was obvious, and I would try to stick as many obviously Jewish words in the grid as I could: PURIM, MENORAH, KOSHER, HAIFA, etc.

But not every entry in a crossword can be Jewish, so I learned to imbue non-Jewish clues with a Hebraic twist. "Slugger Williams" wouldn't do at all for TED, but "Newsman Koppel" was nice. "Andrew Wyeth's field" was far too goyish for ART, but "Robert Rauschenberg's field" was fine (or even "Humorist Buchwald"). DINE was "Nosh classily," ENERGY was "Part of Einstein's equation," NAY was "Barbara Boxer vote," ALUM was "Brandeis grad"— you get the idea.

This might seem cumbersome, but was actually fun. Certain words were a real challenge to "Jewish up," as we labeled this Hebraization process, without seeming too strained. On the entry IOWA, for example, we rejected several lame ideas ("Not very Jewish state," "State seven times

larger than Israel") before hitting paydirt: "State where Ann
Landers was born" (her real name was Esther Lederer).
Bianco and I would brainstorm clues together on the phone,
often spending four or five minutes on a single clue, just to
Jewish it up properly.

But even with the regular income from Puzzle Tov, my
experiment in professional freelancing was proving financially disastrous. I was having to wait too long for checks to
come, sometimes pretending not to have noticed the list of
monthly bills my house's owner had laid out on the kitchen
table, praying that a check would arrive in the day or two I'd
stalled her. Tax time as an independent contractor was a
killer, too—April came and the IRS demanded money I
didn't have.

In the end, the monetary vagaries of the freelancer's life
proved too great. After a year and a half of it, my Visa bill
reached $4,918.40, and I realized it was time to find a more
realistic financial approach to life. My attempt at becoming
a professional crossword puzzle constructor had failed, and
it was time to reassess.

Over the next twelve months, I worked at a camp on the
Chesapeake Bay I'd been a counselor at during previous
summers. It stays open in the off-season for school, church,
and business groups, and living rent and expenses-free
(they provided all meals, housing, and even clothing, if you
didn't mind wearing camp T-shirts all the time, which I
didn't) helped erase the debt I'd accumulated, since it also
gave time for a year's worth of crossword checks to trickle in.
Leading groups of kids on ropes courses and canoeing trips

was a blast, too. Another blast was that a counselor named Lori I'd been friends with finally succumbed to the Gaffney charm (they usually do, believe me), and that spring we moved away from camp together to Annapolis, Maryland. We were a young couple without much of a plan, but in the back of my mind I'd already hatched a new scheme to give professional crossword writing one final shot.

It was my art, and I had missed it during my yearlong break at camp, and I was filled with bitterness that I had been unable to squeeze even a subsistence out of it. I thumbed jealously through books in the crossword sections of bookstores, decrying the unjustness of it all, that I wasn't one of the fortunate few who'd been in the right place at the right time some twenty years before when this or that newspaper was looking for a crossword editor, or who had some other stroke of professional luck that allowed them to earn a living—sometimes a good one—from crosswords. I was just twenty-five, but my crosswords were better than those guys', and knowing that filled me with frustration.

On top of that I was a college dropout, which limited my professional options further. My friends from high school had all gone to big, scary universities, and were now busy at big, scary graduate schools. I had always been something of an academic slacker, though, and during what might have been my college years, I was busy pursuing crosswords, chess, and camp.

So when Lori and I moved to Washington, D.C., in the fall of 1998, this was the last stab as a career that crosswords would get. If it didn't work out, I was going to go back to college, get my degree, and then consider law school.

Since it was a last shot, it had to be a good one. My final attempt would not involve waiting for some editor to die, or hoping to be in the right place when a newspaper made a near-random hiring decision, or networking the big shots and hoping that they'd make an exception in the pecking order for me. Instead, I was going to hustle, to find my own customers.

This was larger than crosswords; it was about what shape my life and personhood would take. I'd always seen myself, as many young people with a certain talent do, as unique, and with a unique skill to share with the wider world. The universe is a harshly efficient place though, and the burden of earning a living usually transforms youthful originality into adult utility.

This is what I was fighting for: my last chance to make the world bend to my will professionally, instead of my bending to fit the world's needs. I felt the pathos of it deeply, and it made me driven, almost desperate.

And so I wrote letters. A lot of letters.

> Dear Editor:
>
> Hello from Washington! I am a professional crossword puzzle constructor and am interested in contributing jazz-themed crosswords to *Jazz Times*. My work has previously appeared in . . .

> Dear Editor:
>
> Hello from Washington! I am a professional crossword puzzle constructor and am interested

in contributing dog-themed crosswords to *Dog Fancy.* My work has previously appeared in . . .

Dear Editor:

Hello from Washington! I am a professional crossword puzzle constructor and am interested in contributing soccer-themed crosswords to *Soccer World.* My work has previously appeared in . . .

Any magazine that looked vaguely possible of publishing a crossword in its pages got a letter from me. Big magazines, like *Sports Illustrated* and *BusinessWeek;* specialty magazines, like *Tennis* and *German Life;* regional magazines like *Chesapeake Life* and *Pennsylvania Today.*

And then one day, the phone rang. It was the editor of *Chesapeake Life* magazine, Pete Nelson. Yes!

"So, we're interested in this crossword thing," he said. "What would it, you know, look like exactly?"

"Well, we could do it pretty much any way you want. I'd make it all about the Chesapeake. Like I was thinking for the first one, if you wanted more than one, that is, I mean, you're under no obligation. But we could make the theme be rivers that flow into the Chesapeake."

"The theme?"

"Yeah. It would be a crossword about rivers that flow into the Chesapeake Bay."

"OK, well that sounds good. What's the cost for one of these?"

I would later learn that pricing is its own art form, but my response at the time was:

"It'd be, well, I'd say we could do it for somewhere around a hundred and fifty, or two hundred dollars, is what we could do. But if that's a problem, you could let me know."

Pretty shaky reply, but it wasn't a problem. He commissioned a first crossword from me for $200. My first direct sale to a magazine, and it paid way more than the *New York Times* pays for their puzzles. No middleman! Hustling was this easy, and I was on my way to making a living at crosswords!

Over the next several months, the following events took place, in this order:

1) I spent six hours creating a very nice Chesapeake Bay rivers-themed crossword puzzle for *Chesapeake Life* magazine;

2) After waiting a few months for the issue with my puzzle in it to come out, I raced to the bookstore and flipped through the magazine. The crossword was not in it;

3) Pete Nelson informed me that, due to space constraints, the puzzle had been pushed off until the next issue;

4) Three months later, the next issue came out, and the puzzle wasn't in it.

5) Pete Nelson wouldn't return my phone messages for several weeks.

6) I finally caught him on the phone at home.

"Matt Gaffney, how are you?"

"Good Pete, you?"

"Oh good, good."

"Great. So yeah, I was wondering about the cr–"

"Yeaaaaah . . . you know, I'm sorry that never worked out. I'm not actually at *Chesapeake Life* anymore . . ."

He then explained how he and the publisher had gotten into it over something, and he'd quit, and that he didn't think they were ever going to publish the crossword, and that he understood I'd done the work that was commissioned and he understood I felt I was owed the $200, and that if I wanted to I could call the publisher and here's his number, but you probably won't get very far.

Never did see that $200. Hustling wasn't going to be easy.

With some perseverance, I wound up getting a few magazines interested in publishing crosswords. They weren't exactly magazines you've heard of, or that I was necessarily proud of having a byline in. As an actor might accept a less-than-glamorous role early in his career, so did I publish crossword puzzles in magazines whose titles might actually make you laugh out loud.

First, there was the *Tabbies* puzzle. Yes, there is a magazine devoted not merely to cats, but to this specific breed of cat. It is filled with stories about tabbies, pictures of them, tips for breeding, and, thanks to me for one 1998 issue, a special tabbies crossword puzzle.

Again, to give an acting analogy, this was the cruciverbal equivalent of an aspiring serious actor accepting a bit part in a Mary-Kate and Ashley Olsen movie. At the top of the page was the puzzle's title, "TABBY TEASER." In between those two words was a picture of a horrified-looking (and not particularly attractive) cat. Underneath, the words "By Matt Gaffney." The chest does swell with pride, does it not? Star answers included MEOW ("Cat's comment"), PETTED ("Stroked kitty"), PAWED ("Touched, cat-style") and STRIPE ("Tabby feature, often").

In keeping with the concept of cluing to the customer I'd learned with Puzzle Tov, some of the clues were fairly clever ways to feline-ize an answer (FEAST was "Cat food brand Fancy ___") while others were sort of stretches (HOLE was "Mouse's escape from the cat") and others were just plain stupid (RENT clued as "Noted Broadway musical—but not "Cats").

The next magazine that bit was something called *UPSCALE* ("The World's Finest African-American Magazine"), followed by *Running Times, German Life*, and then *International Figure Skating*, whose editor commissioned a puzzle, accepted the completed work for publication, then never published and wouldn't return my phone calls or e-mails. Lois Elfman, if you're out there, you still owe me $175, you bitch.

The magazines paid somewhat better (and faster, when they paid) than my old freelance gigs. *Tabbies* paid $205, for instance, *Upscale* paid $240, and *Running Times* $105. These amounts may seem strange and random, and they are. Around that time I developed a pricing theory that if my quoted prices sounded bizarre, like $205, the client wouldn't argue with it. Indeed, I went through several odd pricing theories around this time. Most magazine editors have never run a crossword before, so they have no idea what a reasonable number is. I wasn't sure what to charge them either, so I read up at that time on the science of Naming Your Figure.

In one business book, I read about two brothers who owned a furniture store in the Midwest. They had an interesting and unique three-piece living room set which they priced at $399, which was about standard for a more regular but similarly sized set. It went unsold on their showroom floor for months; many customers looked at it, but eventually found it too weird, and bought more conventional sets for the same price.

Then the brothers had an idea: they were going to position their unique set as a unique set. They doubled the price to $799, and it sold immediately. The higher price had conveyed to the customer what the lower price could not: that these three pieces of furniture were special.

Well, that story got me excited, and I decided to start quoting high prices for my puzzles. The next few bites I got, I quoted the editors prices in the mid-hundreds of dollars. I tried to adopt a tone in my e-mails that made it sound like I didn't care whether they wanted my special brand of crossword or not, but if they did then it was going to cost them, and I had lots of other work to do anyway so if they never called back I didn't care anyway.

Unfortunately, none of them ever called back. It turns out there is only a certain amount that cash strapped editors will pay for crossword puzzles, and perhaps for furniture as well.

I did get one big customer during this period. In August of 1998, I was in a constant state of querying magazines, and a friend gave me a copy *Brill's Content* because there was an article in it about Will Shortz. The piece chronicled Shortz' fabled personal history, and delved into the nuts and bolts of how the *New York Times* crossword gets edited.

In my query letter to *Brill's*, I congratulated them on the article, taking care to point out that Shortz had made several references to a puzzle of mine in the piece, although I wasn't mentioned by name.

They bit. I got a call from Eric Effron, the magazine's managing editor, and a couple of months later, my first puzzle appeared in the magazine.

During my initial conversation with Effron, he naturally asked the big question: how much does one of these crosswords cost? I had tried every pricing trick in the book by that time (tacking a "let me know if that's not doable" on to my quoted price, offering a scale of prices depending on how many they bought, etc.), but I finally learned that, in the end, it all boils down to picking a number you think they can pay and stating it firmly.

Brill's wanted 21 x 21 puzzles, which are large (the size of Sunday *New York Times* puzzles). At that time, the *Times* was paying $350 for such a puzzle, so I decided to go for it, and quoted him $550.

In retrospect, that was a big mistake. I should have asked for at least twice that, and probably more. This was no tiny regional or specialty magazine, but a huge, well-funded national glossy out of New York, and, as with the special set of furniture, quoting the editor a low price merely conveys to him that your work may not be ready for prime time.

But they went for it, and in 1999, my first *Brill's* puzzle appeared. Since it was a media magazine, the puzzles had to be about the press. One was titled "Bill's Story," and featured made-up Bill Clinton quotes about the Monica Lewinsky scandal, which was big news at the time. The theme twist was that each of the faux Clinton quotes ended with the name of a news show. So one clue was "When the dress news came out, I said to Hillary, ___" The answer was I'M VERY SORRY ABOUT TODAY. Another clue was "And though I wanted to hide away forever, ___"—the answer for that one being BUT I HAD TO MEET THE PRESS.

The $550 a month helped, but after five months I got a call telling me the puzzle had been axed (the magazine folded soon thereafter anyway).

I was crushed; with the loss of *Brill's Content,* my goal of becoming a professional crossword writer seemed finished. The small magazines I'd had puzzles in were mostly one- or two-shot deals, and now my one high-paying, consistent gig was gone. I was out of ideas. Obviously going back to freelancing was out of the question.

I was twenty-six years old, and it was time to be realistic. I needed to go back to school, grow up, and get some kind of career rolling. Lori and I had a difficult conversation where we agreed this was the best course of action, although I think letting go of crosswords was even more painful for her than it was for me.

Three days after my conversation with Lori, I received an e-mail. I didn't understand it at first.

It was from Ken Schlager of *Billboard* magazine's Web site. He expressed interest in running a regular online music crossword puzzle.

My first thought was that that was ridiculous. They had misread my e-mail, which was intended to be a query for a crossword in *Billboard*'s print magazine. Technology did exist to solve crossword puzzles online, but why would a specialty magazine like *Billboard* want a crossword on their . . .

On their Web site?

Maybe to increase traffic?

From that misread e-mail, my world shifted. Print magazines had all kinds of complicating factors for freelancers: issues with space, they'd been running the same features for years and were reluctant to change them, and so forth. Why not the brave new world of Web sites, which had few of these limiting problems?

Over the next two weeks I queried over 600 of them, whose focus ran the gamut: sports, politics, music, art, education, science, finance, books, anything. The sentence that kept running through my mind was: "Why the hell didn't I think of this before?" This was 1999, when Web sites had all the money and print magazines were mostly stagnant. I had been scraping the wrong barrel.

It was the golden ticket, the miracle ingredient—the response I got was swift and overwhelming. The Discovery Channel wanted online crosswords on nature; *Slate* magazine wanted a weekly crossword puzzle on politics; *Billboard*'s site wanted their weekly music crossword; the PGA Tour's site wanted a weekly golf crossword; Major League Baseball wanted a monthly baseball puzzle; Motley Fool wanted financial puzzles. Do you have money to pay? We're a Web site, it's 1999, of course we have money to pay. I was charging three or four hundred bucks per puzzle, and cranking them out. It was more work than I could handle alone, so I started a company, pompously named Gaffney Crossword Group, to farm overflow puzzles out to other constructors.

In 1999, I made $12,450 from crossword puzzles, the most I had ever earned in one year. In 2000, my total income from crosswords was over $73,000.

Game over—I was officially a professional crossword puzzle constructor. And I still am, and I still appreciate it, because I'd already had to let it go before it suddenly fell in my lap.

The Internet market has mellowed, of course, but I was able to bank enough to be stable and then move on to other crossword projects. I still get up five mornings (OK, afternoons) a week and make crossword puzzles, and I always like it and occasionally love it, even if I do indulge in griping from time to time. I've branched out into other crossword ventures (see next chapter), but my big break was that I was one of the first constructors to aggressively go after Web sites and offer them custom-made crosswords on any subject, and I was fortunate that that niche was profitable and underserved when I stumbled upon it.

There was clearly some pluck involved in the happy shape my career has taken, but a lot of luck as well. I'll never know which of the two was the decisive factor, and I suppose it doesn't matter. I'm just glad it all turned out the way it did in the end, glad and grateful.

CHAPTER 5

Jonesin'

People who enter this room want one thing, and one thing only: coffee. Before they get to that coffee, though, they have to pass the sharks; I am a shark, and if someone really wants that caffeine fix, they've got to expect a few bites from me.

We're at the twenty-eighth annual convention of the Association of Alternative Newsweeklies, held in June 2005 in San Diego, California. The exhibition room of the Westin Horton Plaza hotel contains twenty-nine booths set up by cartoonists, advice columnists, software companies, tech support firms, and one crossword guy, all hoping to sell their wares to the newspaper editors in attendance. On purpose, the convention organizers have placed a spread containing coffee, juice, muffins, and bagels on the far side of the exhibition room, beyond the booths. Most newspaper editors are more addicted to coffee than they are scared of sharks, so they brave us.

"Ya like crosswords?" I pitch, proffering a paper-clipped batch of puzzle samples.

"No," the stern fiftysomething guy tells me, and keeps walking. I always get a few of these.

"OK," I mutter, but he's already been forgotten since the next editor's about to walk by. You don't count the strikeouts, just the home runs.

"How about some crosswords?" I offer.

"I think we already have a puzzle," the young lady in the aisle tells me. She's an art director, I see from her nametag, so not a decision maker anyway; but it never hurts to hand out the info, so I foist a packet off onto her.

You can tell the ones that really have no intention of buying. Here's one now: a frazzled looking woman in her late forties with grey-streaked black hair and glasses dangling from her neck, with only a couple of minutes to grab coffee and a bagel and rush to her next seminar. You can understand why she doesn't want to be pitched by columnists and cartoonists and the crossword guy: her paper's probably losing money and she's got no space or funds for a new feature, and no time to fall in love with one now besides.

She strides with purpose down the exact center of the aisle, knowing that the slightest glance to her left or right could result in eye contact with the cartoonist who draws "Red Meat" (strip subtitle: "from the Secret Files of Max Cannon") or the sexy redheaded columnist who writes "The Advice Goddess" (the author has appeared on *Politically Incorrect with Bill Maher,* as her promotional literature never fails to point out) or the well-dressed representatives of Classified Technologies Group ("provides classified and display order entry software for weekly newspapers and shoppers in North America"), all of whom are much more eager to talk to her than vice versa.

I'm not even going to bother, but suddenly I hear her name called out:

"Pamela!"

It's a writer whose booth lies across the aisle from mine. His column is called "Kenneth Cleaver: Consumer Correspondent," and Pamela's total sharkbait: they'd had some brief e-mail contact a few months before, it turns out, and now she has to talk to him.

The scent of blood in the water is palpable.

Alternative newsweeklies are those free, superhip papers found in most U.S. cities. Big ones you've probably heard of include the *Village Voice, LA Weekly,* and *Chicago Reader.* Little ones you probably haven't heard of include *Isthmus* (out of Madison Wisconsin, named for the city's dominant geographical feature), *Seven Days* (Burlington, Vermont), and OKC's *Oklahoma Gazette.* Their content tends to be pretty far left, edgy, and sometimes downright shocking, as in the case of syndicated sex columnist Dan Savage, whose "Savage Love" feature often includes references to—well, I'll let you Google "Santorum + Savage" if you wish to know more (and don't say you weren't warned).

In late 2000 I had done a little research and noticed that these newspapers, of which there are several hundred in the U.S. and Canada, did not have a commensurately hip crossword puzzle of their own. Most were running no crossword at all, a few were running the *New York Times* or the *Los Angeles Times,* and several others were running truly terrible syndicated crosswords whose dusky origin I was unable to uncover. At any rate, it seemed to me that they needed a boundaries-pushing puzzle to match the rest of their editorial mix, so I decided to fill that void. It's just the kind of unnoticed niche the budding crossword impresario must always have his antennae tuned to pick up on.

I thought of writing this edgy new crossword feature myself, but doubts crept in. I was never a hipster to begin with, and as my twenties progressed, I felt what small measure of coolness I did possess being slowly sucked out of me. *Law & Order* marathons seemed more and more like a reasonable way to spend Saturday nights; my preferred musical genre, '80s pop, faded in popularity with each passing season; and I'd stopped going to first-run movies long ago since I can't stand people talking and unwrapping cellophane. I was twenty-eight going on ninety, so how could I possibly write a hip weekly crossword puzzle?

I couldn't, but another Matt could: *New York Times*-published crossword author Matt Jones, whom I describe in our early brochures as "a twentysomething, beret-wearin', coffee-drinkin', bands-you've-never-heard-of listenin' hipster from Portland, Oregon. He also happens to be one of the top crossword puzzle constructors in the country."

OK, so he's also a happily married guy who just bought a house and never misses a deadline, but the general audience didn't have to know how upstanding a citizen he actually is. They just needed to know he has his wild side, and that he'd be writing a crossword aimed at the smart, cool, urban set in their twenties and thirties.

So Matt J. came on to write the new feature, and Matt G. would edit his work and sell it to papers. We named it Jonesin' Crosswords, a reference both to Matt's surname and to the fact that crosswords are wicked addictive (drug addicts "jones" for their fix, or want it really bad; the word is used by the hipster crowd to denote any craving, such as "I'm jonesin' for some Cool Ranch Doritos").

Let me put you in someone else's shoes for a moment: imagine being the crossword puzzle editor of a large newspaper. Your boss, the newspaper's editor-in-chief, couldn't care less about the crossword. She knows she has to run one, but couldn't solve the damn thing to save her life, doesn't understand its arcane rules, and has much bigger fish to fry. She's running a newspaper, after all, and your puzzle isn't exactly top priority.

In theory, your main job may be to provide a fun, challenging crossword for solvers, but you're not naive about which side your bread is buttered on. Entertain your solvers with the puzzle? Sure. Educate them? A bit. But your job security lies in keeping things squared with that frazzled editor-in-chief, so what you really fear is not the poorly constructed crossword (how would your editor be able to tell?), or even the occasional factual error sneaking in (hey, stuff happens). No, what keeps you awake at night is the *offended* solver, poison pen in hand, writing letters to your editor-in-chief, threatening to cancel his subscription.

How do these cranky solvers get offended? By words they find offensive lurking in the grid, and even with political correctness reigning o'er the land like a plague of locusts, you'd be surprised at how thin-skinned some people are. *GAMES Magazine* once received a letter complaining that SELES crossed the word STAB in one of their puzzles, a clear and intentional reference, the letter writer felt, to the

near-fatal stabbing of tennis star Monica Seles by a
deranged fan in 1993.

As crossword editor, you're likely to hear from solvers on
two occasions only: when they think you've made a mistake
or when you've caused them offense. Over the years, editors
have tried to avoid the second situation by adopting an
offend-no-one attitude; better a dull clue like "Make non-
functional, casually" for BUST than a possible letter pro-
voker like "Dolly Parton's is prominent."

Needless to say, this walking-on-eggshells mentality
among crossword puzzle editors precluded even the slightest
edginess in crosswords, and for entire generations, American crossword puzzles were pretty much a bowdlerized art
form. CANCER was a no-no in crosswords (and still is, in
many markets), even if innocuously clued as "Sign of the
Zodiac." In some newspapers, the horoscope is printed right
next to the crossword, and one has CANCER in it every day,
while the other never does.

AIDS met a similar fate in the 1980s. The headline of the
newspaper might read "AIDS DEATHS SOAR 200 percent,"
but the crossword puzzle of that newspaper, tucked into a
back page somewhere, was required to be pristine. Even if
clued as "Gives assistance to," AIDS was out. The thinking
was that the crossword puzzle was a sanctum sanctorum, a
place where solvers could go to get away from all the
unpleasant things they might read about in the other parts of
the paper, and was to be left unsullied at all costs.

The thinking was also that the demography of crossword
solvers was primarily elderly women, which was true for a
long time, and still is to some degree. That started to change

in the late 1970s and early 1980s, when the New Wave constructors began to put a little more spice into crosswords, abandoning some of the stodgy puritanism that had ruled since the days of Arthur Wynne.

There is certainly some logic to the cautious approach. Why offend or irritate your readers, after all? Better to shape the puzzle to their sensibilities and tastes, and if certain grid entries will spur them to grab that poison pen, simply leave such entries out. If you want to do the edgier stuff, then, best to take it to the edgier newspapers.

So we did. Jonesin' is the natural (some would say unnatural) extension of the New Wave of the 1970s and '80s in crossword puzzles. As the country slouches towards Gomorrah, Jonesin' provides the edutainment for our collective national trip. That's not exactly true; the puzzle is never gratuitously crude, just far less bound by traditional crossword rules, since our audience is significantly younger than normal puzzle solvers, and, by virtue of picking up an alt-weekly, self-descriptively hip.

Here are some Jonesin' words and clues you won't see in the *New York Times* crossword: GUANO ("Some useful shit"); ORAL SEX ("Activity Bill Clinton sought to define") and MOFO ("Unpleasant character, in slang").

The themes are also on the edge: Matt Jones did one on marijuana puns where "Doobie smoker's campaign style?" was GRASS ROOTS and "Get bigger, spleef-style?" was GROW LIKE A WEED. Another puzzle was titled "Jerry Springer Film Festival," and featured mainstream movies whose titles evoke a *Springer* episode: STRIPTEASE, BREAKDOWN, UNFORGIVEN, and FIGHT CLUB.

Jonesin' was born out of a discrepancy between what I saw with my own eyes and what I had always been told. For my entire crossword career, I'd heard the mantra that the only people who solve crossword puzzles are women in their sixties and seventies, and that, if you wanted to sell a crossword puzzle, it had to be aimed at that market. And then I met Jenn.

As mentioned previously, I worked at a summer camp for a while during the 1990s, and Jenn was a supernaturally attractive counselor who worked at the pool. And oh—she was addicted to crossword puzzles.

I generally go by the theory that if there's one out there of anything, there's probably a lot, so I kept my eyes open, and the idea started to germinate. Why should Jenn have to solve a crossword aimed at people two generations ahead of her? Why should she have to struggle with constant references to Ava Gardner? Or a puzzle that clues ONA with the WWI slang "Three ___ match"? Or a puzzle that clues CLOONEY as "Singer Rosemary" instead of "George of *O Brother, Where Art Thou*?" She can't name an Ava Gardner movie, or tell you what "Three on a match" means (the idea was that matches were scarce, so when lighting cigarettes, soldiers should aim to light three of them with a single match), or sing a Rosemary Clooney song.

And once I started looking for them, I saw more. When I moved to DC, they were everywhere—twentysomethings solving crosswords in coffeehouses, on the bus, in the dog park. And it got more and more obvious that there was a niche.

I Googled my way to the existence of the annual convention of the Association of Alternative Newsweeklies, which was to be held that summer in New Orleans just a couple of short months away. I signed up in a hurry, and before I knew it was on a plane down to the Big Easy to hawk hip puzzles.

Two weeks before the convention, I got a phone call. It was from a guy I'll call Marcus Young, editor of a small alt-weekly on the West Coast I'll call the *Pacific Explainer*. Marcus wanted to run Jonesin', and we settled on $15 per week. First sale! I hung up the phone and jumped around the apartment pumping my fist in the air with maximum glee; at least I'd be heading down to the convention with one paper in tow, so now I could tell prospective buyers that the puzzle appeared somewhere besides my imagination.

But alternative weeklies tend towards financial instability. Two years later, the *Pacific Explainer* shuttered its doors without ever having paid any part of their bill. They owed Jonesin' close to $2,000, but there was nothing I could do.

Non-payment has been an issue with Jonesin' from the start. Alternative weeklies are usually labors of love, started by middle-aged editors who want an exciting career change, wealthy older people who want a meaningful place to spend their pile, or fresh-from-college, idealistic kids who think their town lacks a lefty voice and start up a paper on a shoestring budget. Many of the independents make little or no money; many lose money. The larger chains make a bundle, most notably the seventeen-paper New Times Media/*Village Voice* chain (yes, the original alt-weekly is now the flagship paper of a chain of corporate alt-weeklies). These chains are in the black primarily because they have more skilled management, work on economies of scale, and attract more national advertising than the smaller, independent papers.

It's not uncommon for alternative newsweeklies to fold after a couple of years—or a couple of months, or a couple of issues—and in the period just before one of them closes for good, making payroll for their employees is more pressing than paying the syndicated crossword service located 2,000 miles away. Which means that Jonesin' sometimes winds up holding the bag.

Like animals able to sense an earthquake before it happens, I've learned to tell when an alternative newsweekly is about to shutter its doors. I normally invoice once every six months—probably not a wise policy since it lets papers slide by for a long time before I notice they're having financial issues, but that's how I do it. About 60 percent of papers cough the dough up right away, and I see the check within a couple of weeks. The deadbeats get a friendly reminder, which usually shakes the cash out of most of them. Anyone left over gets a third, less-than-friendly reminder. If I don't get a check within a week after that, I know the paper's going under. There's not much to be done at that point, though, except maybe a last-ditch plea for partial payment, which extracts a couple hundred pity dollars about 10 percent of the time. But anyone who works with alternative newsweeklies eventually comes to terms with a cold fact: eating accounts receivable money is just part of doing business with this crowd.

It's a fun crowd, though. My second sale of Jonesin' came in New Orleans; in the evenings, the host newspaper (New Orleans' *Gambit Weekly*, that year) sets up wild events at bars or other local venues for nametag wearing convention-eers to get drunk and schmooze at. I didn't know anyone at the convention, but my outgoing demeanor combined well with three Heinekens and an obscure piece of Eastern European trivia to rack up sale #2.

I spotted a young, preppily-dressed, attractive couple standing by the bar looking somewhat out of place; it seemed as though they didn't know anyone at the convention, either. His name was Blair and hers was Stephanie, their nametags told me, and their last name read BARNA.

"Hey," I called out, swaggering up to them, "that means 'brown' in Hungarian."

Blair's face lit up. "It sure does," he said. "Now, how the hell did you know that?" Spent a little time in Hungary a few years ago, I told him. We talked for a half hour and later got lost going to a strip club on Bourbon Street. Two weeks later they became Jonesin's second customer.

Later at the convention, I took about seventy-five papers set up along display tables by the far wall and schlepped them back to the friend's house I was staying at. I spent a couple of hours going through each paper to see which of them ran a crossword and which didn't, and which puzzle they ran if they did have one. Valuable information, since it's best to target papers that don't already carry a puzzle (or that carry a weak puzzle).

The convention was held in the Ritz-Carlton in New Orleans, a city so blighted by urban decay that the convention guidebook carried a full-page of "Advice from the NOPD," such as "ignore anyone who wants to show you where the action is or wants to lead you to a club or bar" and

"If you are robbed, remain calm. Do not try to run. Do not beg for your life." A few nights later, the friend I was staying with, an ER doctor doing his residency, told us of a case that had come in that night—a young Swedish tourist beaten within an inch of his life by a kid who'd lured him out of the safety of the French Quarter to buy pot.

But that was outside; inside, I set myself up in the booth right across from Stephen Notley, a Canadian cartoonist who draws an absurdist strip called "Bob the Angry Flower" (book title: *In Defence of Fascism*). The plot of each strip involves an irascible, omnipotent sunflower named Bob getting mad at some aspect of life and destroying the world, or reacting in some other malevolent fashion.

Just before the convention started, I had done a quick trip around the exhibition hall to see what other kinds of people and companies were there, and was pleased to spot a bearded man in a Hawaiian shirt walking around with a Jonesin' brochure he'd gotten off my display table. I assumed he was a newspaper editor who'd snuck in a few minutes before the doors officially opened; could this be sale #3?

A few minutes later my body froze in horror: there was the Hawaiian shirt guy sitting behind a booth . . . hawking his own hip crosswords to people there!

He was representing a new syndicate called "Sweeping Features" that specialized in content for the alternative press. I quickly solved their sample crossword and realized it was terrible; many of the down words weren't even words, but gobbledygook left unclued (you can't do that!). Later I went over to the guy's table and asked where he'd had his crosswords published previously.

He knew he'd been caught frontin' and muttered, "I've never had a crossword published anywhere before." Busted, but could I make the case to harried newspaper editors who don't know anything about crosswords and don't care?

I spent the rest of the convention having those editors ask me what the difference was between Jonesin' and the Sweeping Features puzzle, and explaining the errors in that puzzle to them. In the end, it worked; I got a few more customers to sign up for Jonesin', and two years later, Sweeping Features was out of business (both the syndicate and its crossword). I hate to see anyone go under; I'm really a nice guy. But Hawaiian Shirt was stepping on my territory without the right creds, so I'm not too ashamed to say that I'm glad he got the eventual hook.

Selling crosswords: don't let anyone tell you it's not dog-eat-dog.

Pitching a no-hitter blindfolded. Sailing around the world in a plastic kiddie pool. Winning Powerball twice in a week. This is a list of feats easier to accomplish than getting a newspaper to switch its old crossword puzzle for a new one.

Alright, I'm exaggerating—but not by much. A newspaper's editor in chief wants primarily to hear that nothing about the crossword except that no one's upset about it, and the idea of changing crosswords unless it's absolutely necessary is anathema. It's a lot of effort, generally evokes a ton of angry reader mail, and in the end, usually results in a quick switch back to the original puzzle, whose position then becomes more secure than ever.

But Jonesin' pulled it off once—and we did it against the *New York Times*.

I won't lie—this technique fails way more often than it succeeds. It's gotten to the point where I tell editors who already run a puzzle not to bother switching—it'll just cause them hassle, and me hassle, so now I just pitch Jonesin' to papers without any puzzle at all.

And we failed before we succeeded, too. I'd had a couple of papers try to switch from the *Times* to Jonesin' before, but each switch lasted only a week. Alternative weeklies in Boise, Idaho, and Columbia, South Carolina, told me the same thing—they'd tried to make the change, but readers had complained so vociferously that they'd felt they had no choice but to change back, even though the editors themselves agreed that Jonesin' fit their editorial mix better than the *Times* puzzle.

But why talk about failure when there's a success story to relate?

The showdown site was Eugene, Oregon, where the *Eugene Weekly* had run the *New York Times* puzzle for around ten years. I knew from experience that this was going to be a hard battle to win, maybe impossible. People get used to the style, tone, and difficulty level of whatever crossword puzzle they regularly solve, so woe be unto any editor who replaces their puzzle with a new one. This is true even if the puzzle is objectively not very good, but it's especially true of an excellent puzzle like the *New York Times*.

After my experiences with Boise and Columbia, I began to warn editors who switched that the change would ultimately be good for them, but that they should expect a few dozen angry calls and e-mails at first. People got used to their crossword, I explained, but would soon take to Jonesin's hipness and forget all about that boring old *Times* puzzle (I don't actually find the *Times* puzzle boring, but that's the salesman in me talking).

Eugene Weekly's editor Ted Taylor rode the storm out for a few months. The calls persisted, however, so he decided to let his readers decide: he announced in the *Weekly* that the paper was taking a reader poll, and whichever puzzle got more reader support would run, while the other would get axed.

At first the *Times* was ahead, but Jonesin' pulled even later in the race, and the pure zeal of the letters in support of Jonesin' convinced Taylor to stick with the puzzle. One letter writer opined: "I am also writing as a crossword addict. So, on the question of running the Jonesin' or the *NYT* crossword, I say: Jonesin! Jonesin! Jonesin! PLEASE keep the Jonesin' crossword! Its irreverence is refreshing. Besides, *The Oregonian* runs the *NYT* crossword every day! I don't know if the *R-G* runs it or not, but I implore you to keep me Jonesin'!"

And now that the puzzle's ensconced in Eugene, it'll never get kicked out. The same forces that work against you can also be made to work on your behalf.

Merl Reagle was the first to do it in the 1980s, and the *New York Times* followed in 1998, and then Stan Newman did one in *Newsday.* And in 2005, it was Jonesin's turn to get a couple engaged via crossword puzzle.

It involved the *Eugene Weekly* again. *EW* reader Dan

O'Reilly didn't just want to say "Will you marry me?" to his girlfriend, Angela Turner. He wanted to say "W_ _ L Y_ U _ _ R R Y M _?" to his girlfriend, A _ G _ _ A T_ R _ _R.

Dan and Angie solve the Jonesin' puzzle together every week, so Dan figured that instead of simply going down on one knee and strapping a nice rock to her finger, he'd ask Angie to be his betrothed via their weekly crossword.

Dan got in touch with me and I told him it sounded like fun. He sent me details about Angie and her life, and I forwarded them along to Matt J., who crafted them into the Jonesin' puzzle that ran in *EW,* June 23 of 2005.

To 99.99 percent of the people who solved that week's puzzle in alternative weeklies across the country, it just seemed like a normal crossword. But to one Oregon couple, it was filled with hidden meanings. In addition to having ANGELA at 1-across (clued as "Tony's housemate on *Who's the Boss?*"), the puzzle had TURNER as the corresponding last across answer in the grid (clued as "Spatula, essentially").

In the center of the grid, two across entries read WILL YOU and MARRY ME. In addition, the grid included the hopeful groom's name (DAN and O'REILLY), as well as various other aspects of Angie's life—all of them clued in a straightforward, non-Angie-specific way.

How did the groom's scheme go down? I'll let him pick up the action:

> *Day started off with Angie arriving in Corvallis around 11 AM, all prepared for a trip to the Rogue brewery for their summer garage sale. We took off*

for Newport, grabbed a bite to eat at this hole in the wall restaurant called the Chowder Bowl, then headed for the Rogue, where somehow I must have confused the dates of the garage sale by a week. Not one to leave empty handed, we grabbed a 22 oz. bottle of some of their finest to enjoy on the beach. After picking a spot, we laid down a blanket and whipped out the EW to enjoy the crossword and the sunshine. First answer she got was 1-Across "Angela." We had completed about half the puzzle when she worked on down to "Turner," where she mentioned (this is verbatim from her mouth), "Hey this puzzle has both of my names in it, we should keep it when we're finished!" It was at this point that she was just as surprised to find both of my names in the puzzle as well; must be a coincidence!

"We worked on the puzzle for about a half-an-hour when we started to slow down. I asked her if she was done working on it and she said yes, to which I replied that I didn't think she was. At this point, I'm looking straight at the puzzle where it says, "WILL YOU MARRY ME" with my pencil right next to the phrase. After not getting the subtle hint, I told her that maybe I could help her finish the puzzle, which is when I took a Sharpie marker and circled the answers ANGELA TURNER WILL YOU MARRY ME. She was absolutely dumbfounded, almost to the point of embarrassment that she didn't see it while we were

> *working on it! After an initial whisper of "Oh my*
> *God," her first complete sentence was, "There*
> *never was a garage sale today, was there?"*

In case you're wondering: She said a three-letter word for "I agree."

See? Jonesin' isn't all hard edges and sarcasm. Deep down, it's a crossword with a soft spot.

What makes Matt Jones' puzzles so gosh darn edgy? I think it's the particular shape of his brain, or maybe he was dropped on his head as an infant and that did it. Editing Matt's work is an angst-ridden joy. I sit down to solve the crossword each Friday, and slowly a word will start to emerge, and I'll think, "Oh, he couldn't have put that in there . . ." and a few more letters will come into place, and I'll realize that he did, in fact, put that in there. And I'll get the vapors.

Matt is particularly good at coming up with themes that highlight oddball anomalies in our everyday language; I didn't really know it was possible for a crossword to provide social commentary before I started editing his puzzles. In one, entitled "You Already Said That!" Matt chronicles redundancies that will not die: ATM MACHINE, PAST HIS-TORY, FEW IN NUMBER, END RESULTS, and the double-barreled EXTRA ADDED BONUS. Another memorable theme used phrases that include a pierceable body part: RAISE AN EYEBROW, RUBBER NIPPLE (ouch), FOREIGN TONGUE, NAVEL ORANGES, HAD A NOSE FOR NEWS. Yet another included six of the seven deadly sins: PRIDE AND JOY, ANGER MANAGEMENT, TREE SLOTH, PENIS ENVY, HAS A LUST FOR LIFE, and GREED IS GOOD (yes, including the seventh sin would've made the theme perfect, but neither of us could think of a phrase with GLUTTONY in it, so that was that).

Matt's clues also tend to be not-quite-ready-for-the-mainstream: IGUANA is "Pet of many hipsters"; "Hairstyle that may have a comb in it" for AFRO; and "Give a rat's ass" for CARE.

As of this writing, Jonesin' Crosswords appears in fifty-four newspapers around the U.S. and Canada. As the papers it runs in are labors of love for their owners, so is Jonesin' something of a labor of love for Matt J. and me as well. Neither of us makes a mint off it, but it's enjoyable and we're attached to it. Matt J. likes corrupting the nation's youth with a twisted crossword every week, and I enjoy selling his work; after five years, it's still a sharp thrill when a new paper e-mails or calls to say they want to buy.

Any labor of love has its moments when you know it's all been worth it. For Jonesin', it was this 2005 e-mail:

> Hi,
> Just want to say I love your puzzles and have done every one since they started publishing in the Cleveland Ohio *Free Times*. I have been a crossword lover my whole life. These are so unique and fun, they have even enticed my husband into completing them with me weekly. Friday night is our "puzzle" night to complete your puzzle. We look forward to it.

This past week's puzzle has stumped us, however, and the answers are not posted on the Free-
times Web site. The one we are stuck on is 20
across—Memo header about someone doing a
second scan? I hate to give in, but have been
puzzling since Friday and cannot get this one.
Help !! thanks a lot.

(P.S. Don't know if this gives you a story about
how your puzzles are completed, but we are
naturists (nudists) for a long time. We belong to a
club/camp and do them Fri evenings in either
our trailer or at the hot tub. Of course, always in
the nude. Usually with a good refreshment. The
perfect relaxation after a week of work.)

                                                D & A

Let's see someone try that with a *New York Times* crossword. Bring it on, Shortz! Yeah, I didn't think so.

CHAPTER 6

Are Humans Necessary?

Once a month, Frank Longo packages up a data-jammed CD and inserts it into a mailbox. Posted from Jersey City, it lands a day or two later at what Longo calls an "undisclosed location," where it gets tossed onto a stack with all the other CDs from previous months.

Longo hopes never to need that stack, but sleeps better at night knowing it's there, since each CD contains a fully updated copy of his crossword entry database. It's unique, it's taken Longo ten years to compile, and it's valuable. "If my apartment building burns down, I don't want to lose my database," Longo explains. "It's my bread and butter. It's my livelihood."

Yes, there are commercial data preservation services available, but in the relatively low-tech world of crossword puzzle constructing, Longo's makeshift system passes for a Tom Clancy operation. So maybe the "undisclosed location" is just a friend's garage in suburban Maryland, but who cares? Longo's got the biggest database in crosswords, so you'd better believe he wants to protect it.

"I am a completist," Longo tells me over dinner in the

West Village. "For example, if I have"—here he taps his head—"what's the capital of Nevada?"

"Carson City."

"OK, right. So if I added Carson City to my database, then I'd have to add all the other forty-nine state capitals, too."

But that's an easy example, since Longo's 720,000-entry database certainly contains words as obvious as the state capitals. A tougher example, also state based: Longo recently noticed that the three letters denoting the political affiliation and home state of governors, senators, and members of congress, such as "D-MA" for Ted Kennedy or "R-UT" for Orrin Hatch, open up several dozen new three-letter entries for cruciverbalists. Some of them are already cluable as words, like Hatch's R-UT, which is just the word "rut," but most are totally new combinations, like D-SD or R-AL.

I challenge Longo on whether these should really be legit entries in a crossword—constructors debate endlessly over whether a particular entry is too contrived to use in a puzzle or not—but Longo just grins. "You see these all the time on TV, R-DE and stuff like that," so into his database they went. In his completist fashion, Longo added all 100 possible (major party + state abbreviation) combinations to his list, minus the R-UT-like overlaps that were already valid entries anyway.

Computers have changed almost everything in the past few decades, and how crossword puzzles get written is one of them. There are three parts to constructing a crossword: coming up with a theme, filling the grid, and writing the clues. Until artificial intelligence makes some serious leaps, humans will continue to do the heavy lifting on parts one and three. HAL of *2001: A Space Odyssey* fame might've been able to come up with tricky, original, theme-worthy wordplay and fresh, ingenious clues, but nothing we've got today outside of a Hollywood fantasy can actually do that, any more than a computer can write a short story or even a joke. Databases can help sort and track clues—letting an editor avoid repeating a certain clue, for instance—but that's about as far as it goes.

So themes and clues are still human territory for the foreseeable future, but the second part, filling grids with words, is far more cyber-friendly a task than the other two, and it's here that computers have revolutionized the construction of crossword puzzles.

In 1989, a young computer scientist from Boston named Eric Albert needed a new career. He and his wife had decided to have a child, and it made more economic sense for her to continue working and him to watch the baby. "I needed a job where I could pick my own hours and use my skills," Albert tells me.

That summer he attended the national convention of a word and math puzzle society, and saw how many people made puzzles as a hobby. He wondered if crossword constructing in particular might be not just a hobby, but a semi-lucrative career.

"The people at the convention said no way. I asked them, what if I used a computerized generator to write crosswords much faster than a person could? Would I make a living at it then? They said it was theoretically possible, but that computers can't generate crosswords. I told them, I'm the computer scientist, that's my problem."

He wrote the first version of his program in thirteen hours in August of 1989. It spat out some marginal 3 x 4 grids, but nothing that would be commercially viable. Albert checked out the academic literature and found a paper written by four MIT computer scientists stating that only a few crude crossword-filling programs had ever been devised, and that they did not produce quality grids, but rather grids full of obscure words, as Albert's thirteen-hour attempt had.

Then Albert had an insight: a computer could generate high-quality crossword puzzles if each entry in its database was ranked on, say, a scale from one to ten. An excellent puzzle word like JUKEBOX might be worth a 9 or 10, while an obscurity like UNAU (a type of sloth that appears in crosswords more often than it should) would be a 1 or a 2. That way, the junk would be left out, and just the good stuff would go in. The only problem was that no such ranked database existed, so Albert set out to create one. He began by merging computerized versions of several unabridged dictionaries. Then he added a large number of non-dictionary but in-the-language phrases that make excellent crossword entries (such as SEE YA and NO CAN DO) and pop culture references like movies, TV shows, and well-known songs.

Then he began the laborious process of ranking the words, one by one. He used a scale from 0 to 12, where 0 meant a "fabulous" word, according to Albert, while 12 meant an entry that was, as he terms it, "very yucky." Over the next three years, Albert gave a ranking to every 3-, 4-, 5-, 6-, 7-, 8-, and 9-letter word in the abridged dictionaries' list, plus those in his added words lists.

His database consisted of an astonishing 250,000 ranked

words, and Albert was having great success in publishing his work (I remember seeing his puzzles for the first time in magazines around then, and marveling over how wide open and clean his grids were—and how prolific he was). Fearing anti-computer backlash, Albert told no one in crosswords that the puzzles he was publishing to rave reviews were actually the work of a grid fill program; only after establishing a name for himself and his work did he reveal the assistance of his computer and database. "I have never in my life created a crossword puzzle by hand," he claims. "I would have no idea how to do it."

People seemed more intrigued than annoyed by the possibility of computer-generated grids, though, and Albert's career was soaring—until a different kind of computer backlash struck.

It was in the early fall of 1991 that he first began to feel soreness in his wrist. He didn't think much of it, but then in November, Albert says: "I woke up one morning and my wrist hurt a lot—and it didn't stop hurting for years."

He never got a precise diagnosis, but it was "some combination of repetitive stress disorders accumulated over time. I'm certain its cause was rating up to 1,000 words a day for several hundred days in a row."

Whatever it was, it spelled the end of Albert's revolutionary list. Following the diagnosis, he quit rating words, but continued to perform the less wrist-taxing task of creating and selling puzzles using the words he'd already keyed in and ranked. "People with chronic pains still have to pay their mortgages," he explains, "and this was the career that I had built."

Albert made some changes in his life—got an ergonomic

chair, read books in a book holder instead of holding them in his hands—and continued creating puzzles throughout the 90s. Without a continually expanding pool of entries, though, his list's functionality diminished over time. Over various rights issues, Albert stopped creating and selling puzzles in 1999, and now keeps only a toehold in the cross-word world, focusing more on creative writing and other projects these days.

"In 1989, the hardware available for running this was a joke," he says. "You really did have to be a computer scientist to get a computer anywhere close to producing a good grid."

But technological progress does not rely on one man alone. Since Albert's injury and semiretirement from puz-zles, the computer-aided construction gauntlet has been picked up and expanded on by others such as Longo, Peter Gordon, and a Delaware constructor named Bob Klahn. People don't often talk about it, still fearing a stigma, but it's now generally believed that the majority of top crossword writers—perhaps a supermajority—use computer-aided design to some degree in constructing their grids.

The two tools you need for this are Crossword Compiler and a database. Luckily the first comes with the second— plunk down $49 for the industry standard Crossword Com-piler program and you get a bunch of word lists tossed in free. Be prepared to do some pruning before you send your Crossword Compiler database–produced work to editors, though; its programmer has included lists laden with ultra obscurities (MIRFAK, PANGA, COYPU) as well as a slew of X-rated entries that would render a puzzle unprintable in most markets (WHOREMASTER and WHOREMONGER being among my favorites; "Honey, what's an eleven-letter word for . . . ?").

So where can you get a quality database for a low price? For years you couldn't, as pioneers in the field like Albert and Longo carefully guarded their self-ranked word lists. And why wouldn't they? The several thousand dollars they could have earned from selling their lists would be like killing the goose that lays the golden eggs, since database sellers would soon find themselves competing with database buyers on the puzzle market. It was a loophole in the capitalist fabric that kept good word lists from being sold, since it was economically irrational for anyone in possession of a quality database to sell it.

Until recently, that is, when Kevin McCann changed much of that. McCann is a friendly, middle-aged Ottawa resident who runs cruciverb.com, the most prominent Web site devoted to crossword puzzle construction. It's where experienced constructors and newbies alike hang out to discuss puzzle-writing strategy, ask for advice, and kibitz on recently published puzzles.

In 2003, McCann made available on his site a database of all entries that had been published in puzzles in prominent U.S. newspapers. Once an entry appeared in a *Los Angeles Times* or *Newsday* or *New York Times* crossword, onto McCann's master list it went. If it was good enough for a puzzle editor at one of those papers, the logic went, it must be a quality entry.

Such databases had previously been under the purview of that handful of hardcore constructors who had engineered their own similar lists, but then they became suddenly available for only a small membership fee at McCann's site. There weren't any apparent legal issues, individual crossword clues being uncopyrightable, so a non-constructor could suddenly throw down $49 for Crossword Compiler, plus a nominal fee to McCann, and *voila*—a human constructor wasn't really necessary anymore.

Or so it was feared, though it turned out to be not quite true. Getting a truly high-quality grid still "definitely involved an interaction between the human and the computer," according to Longo. But it also made it so that pretty good-quality grids were now available for mere chump change, plus some human tweaking. Not quite publishable puzzles, perhaps, except for lower-end magazines, but still not bad at all.

Although "Kevin McCann's lists have changed the game," as Longo puts it, private lists like Longo's still have great value, especially on higher-end puzzles. The weakness of McCann's list is that it includes any entry that has made it into one of the top U.S. newspaper puzzles, but fails to differentiate between good and bad words the way ranked lists do. So if a lousy word like ESNE has made it into, say, the *New York Times* crossword even once in the past several years, which it has, McCann's database treats it the same as a great entry like EXXON or KOJAK. Over time, such lousy words, if left unpruned, grow to crowd the good entries like kudzu vines squeezing the local flora. If it doesn't know any better, after all, your computer will stick ESNE in every other puzzle you tell it to make.

To keep ahead of McCann, Longo is constantly updating his list, adding all #1 songs as they emerge, visiting the Internet Movie Database every few weeks to key in new movies and stars and directors, and adding novel phrases as he comes across them in life or while instant messaging with friends. His laptop almost seems like an extension of his person, ready to be slipped out and called into service as effortlessly as a reporter takes out his notepad.

Longo has spent the past decade doing this, and his database should hit a million entries in the next couple of years. Roughly half of the words on his list are ranked, while the other half are raw dictionary database entries that may or may not be gridworthy. It's the largest ranked database in all of crosswords, and has earned him demigod status among puzzle folk. At the 2005 American Crossword Puzzle Tournament I watched one evening as competitors gathered around Longo and his laptop and played a game one described to me as "Stump Frank's Database." Someone would call out a word or phrase, such as DO-RAG, and Frank would type it in to see if it was in there, which it usually was. Having ranked the entries himself, Longo knows his list well—even before typing a shouted-out entry in to check, he usually gave a preliminary "I know I have that" or "I don't think I've got that," and he was usually right.

Databases are valuable and not shared lightly; and wherever there are computer geeks, rivalries develop. While I'm discussing computer-aided grid fills with Peter Gordon at his home, an impish grin breaks across his face. "I have a four-letter word in my database that I know Frank doesn't have," he tells me. "It's not a great word, but it's totally usable."

"Can you tell me what it is?" I ask.

"I can tell you," he replies sternly, "but you can't tell Frank. I don't want to see this word in one of his puzzles next month."

The word turns out to be ASNE, the first name of Norwegian journalist ASNE Seierstad, who wrote the bestselling

The Bookseller of Kabul. As Gordon said, it's not a great entry by any stretch, but when you're working in the rarefied world of legitimate four-letter words that don't appear in Frank Longo's database, it's gold.

The attentive reader will have noticed by now that Peter Gordon is a hypercompetitive individual, so it should come as no surprise that he claims to have a better database than Longo's. The two have an unspoken rivalry as possessing the two best word lists in crosswords, and they indeed use them in the service of the two best daily crosswords in the country, the *New York Sun* (Gordon is its editor) and the *New York Times* (Longo does occasional grid fixes for Will Shortz).

Gordon's database, like Longo's and Albert's before that, began with a dictionary's electronic database, and now includes 194,000 words, 121,000 of which have been ranked on a scale from 1 to 100. That's far fewer entries than Longo's, but Gordon's ranking system is more refined: he ranks his words not on a scale from 1-10 based mostly on feel, as Longo does, but on a scale of 1-100, with certain specified parameters necessary for a word to qualify in a given range. For a word to rank in the 90s, it has to be both a quality phrase and have at least one rare letter, like MAIN SQUEEZE or TV QUIZ SHOW. To rank in the 80s, it has to be a common word with a rare letter, or a nice phrase without a rare letter, like KAZOO or K-MART. A word like PURGES goes in the 50s—"there's definitely something wrong" with an entry in the 50s, Gordon notes, the "wrong" thing here being that it ends in an S (yes, that's somewhat nitpicky to dock points from a word simply because it's pluralized, but it's fair). Entries in the 40s range are generally partials like IT IN (clued as "Get ___ writing!"), for example. Anything under 40 Gordon deems as "unusable," though he'll manually slum in the 30s on occasion to fill out an otherwise nice corner.

When he's got his theme entries placed in the grid, Gordon assesses where the black squares should go (this is instinct, based on his general feel of what the computer can handle and what it can't). Then he'll set it to fill based on a fairly high minimum word value, say 60. This means the computer will try to fill the grid only with entries that are valued at 60 or above; if it can't do it, Gordon reshuffles a few black squares to make the computer's task easier and tries again, or he simply lowers the minimum entry number a bit, to 55 or so, and sees if the computer can tackle that, which it probably can. Such grids usually take the computer less than a minute to fill.

Longo doesn't mind writing his grids largely by computer, since he knows how to do it by hand, which many contemporary puzzle writers don't. "There's a fundamental issue of whether you know how to do it by hand," he says. "It becomes an ethical issue." As noted in Chapter 2, Will Shortz agrees with this, and so do I, but Peter Gordon doesn't. Though he used to write puzzles by hand himself, it doesn't bother him if a cyber-aided constructor never learned how. When I ask him about the ethics of that, he just throws his hands up in the air as if to say that you can't stop the world from turning. Which is true, of course, but I don't have to like it.

After all this, the obvious question arises: who can write a better crossword grid, the best humans or the best computers?

To answer that, I arranged for two top human constructors
to take on Longo and Gordon's databases in a pair of set
crossword constructing tasks—the Ultimate Crossword
Smackdown, if you will. Then I asked a panel of highly-
respected judges to rate the results—without knowing which
puzzles were human-written and which computer-written—
and devised a simple scoring system to quantify the tally.

Would silicon top gray matter in this battle, or vice versa?
The general sense among participants was that the computers would carry the day, but that we carbon-based life
forms indeed had a fighting chance.

To represent humanity in this battle, I humbly chose
myself as one of the participants, then tapped Byron Walden
as my teammate. The reader will recall Walden as the constructor of the infamously difficult Round 5 puzzle at the 2006
Stamford tournament chronicled in Chapter One. The forty-
two-year-old is indeed one of the top constructors in the
country—and, notably, one of the dwindling few who (like me)
doesn't use a grid-filling program to write his puzzles. Open a
volume of *New York Times* or *New York Sun* puzzles and you're
likely to see Walden's byline on the best puzzle in the book;
the easygoing, blond-haired Californian is a transplanted
Kentucky native who spends his non-puzzlemaking hours as a
professor of mathematics at Santa Clara University.

Representing computers ("boooo!"), we have the data-
bases/computers of Frank Longo and Peter Gordon, who by
now need no introduction.

Our distinguished judges: Ellen Ripstein, 2001 ACPT
champion and professional puzzle editor; Tyler Hinman,
2005 and 2006 ACPT champion; Trip Payne, three-time

ACPT champion and one of the top constructors in the country for the past two decades; Jon Delfin, seven-time ACPT champion (owner of more ACPT titles than anyone else, in fact); and Rich Norris, editor of the *Los Angeles Times* crossword and, like Payne, one of the top constructors in the country for roughly the past twenty years.

The two tasks the four competitors have to complete are as follows: first, fill in a 5 x 6 corner of a grid with one unchangeable word already filled in (see grid A); and second, fill in a standard, 15 x 15 crossword puzzle grid with three 15 x 15 theme entries already placed, unchangeable and unmovable (see grid B).

GRID A

GRID B

The time limit for the two tasks is set at two days; though the computers are likely to finish faster than the humans, this is not important to the ultimate solver, who doesn't know whether the puzzle took a human twenty hours or a computer twenty seconds to fill. The only important thing in this battle is the quality of the end product.

Is it possible for Byron and me to beat the Longo/Gordon database juggernauts? It's possible, we feel, but we'll need to use a little "strategy."

When Garry Kasparov faced IBM computer Deep Blue in 1996 for the (unofficial, but de facto) World Chess

Championship, he had to veer significantly from his usual style. Against fellow humans, Kasparov goes for head-spinning tactics and open positions, playing exciting openings like the Gruenfeld Defense and Sicilian Defense. He knows he can out-calculate any human he comes across, so he's not afraid of hand-to-hand combat with pieces flying all over the board. He rarely loses such battles.

Against Deep Blue, however, Kasparov would rarely, perhaps never, win such a tactical fight, and he knew it. Turning the game into a riotous melee would be stepping right into the computer's strong point, brute force calculation. Instead, Kasparov altered his playing style considerably against Deep Blue, opting for slow, drawn-out, rather boring strategic battles. In this type of chess game, the computer's ability to calculate concrete variations is less useful; instead, the position calls for judgment, long-range planning, recognition of superior pawn structures, and other more abstract concepts than the crude "if-he-does-this-then-I'll-do-that" sort of process the computer excels at. Kasparov beat the computer using precisely this strategy, though Deep Blue did manage to exact revenge in a future match.

If Byron and I are going to beat the comps, we're going to have to pursue a similar course, focusing on stuff that humans do well but computers don't. We're going into this as John Henrys, more or less realizing the handwriting is on the wall: at some point in the future, computers will do this better than humans, but are we there yet? It's also humbling to realize that the main reason we aren't there yet (if we're not) is because, unlike IBM with Deep Blue, there isn't a multi-billion dollar company pumping funds into computerizing this task. Crossword Compiler was written in the spare time of an English graduate student in astrophysics, Antony Lewis; the database work is being done piecemeal by several competing editors, like Longo and Gordon, who have little to gain from sharing their information toward a common goal, and neither is a programmer himself.

So humility is in the air, as well as caveats about how subjective the judges' decisions will be, and so forth. But winning, I assure you, is very much on everyone's mind—or central processing unit, as it were.

I start with the 5 x 6 task. A 5 x 6 block is fairly challenging for a crossword writer to fill, but not annoyingly so—I know I'll probably wind up with several different finished 5 x 6 grids to choose from, so this part of the contest will boil down to an editorial decision as much as it will a constructing one. Again, the five unchangeable letters jutting into the grid are MOSQU, from the longer entry MOSQUITO COAST, so the Q makes this more interesting than if the letters had been, say STORE or UNDER or something less Scrabble-riffic. My first thought is: is it possible to get a good fill with another rare letter (X, Q, Z or J) in it besides the pre-placed Q? If so, that'd be a strong contender. My second thought is: is it possible to use an entry where the pre-placed Q isn't followed by a U? The judges would probably like that, so

I set off to fill my corner with those two artistic guidelines in the back of my mind.

As I begin work, another reality dawns on me that supersedes concerns about rare letters and Q being followed by a U: I realize that I've got to use at least one entry that Peter and Frank's databases don't have. Since there are no additional black squares permitted and everyone has the same area to fill, failing to come up with at least one virginal word will mean that in order to beat the comps, this daunting series of events would have to take place: I'd have to come up with a grid Frank and/or Peter themselves find, but reject in favor of a different grid—and then the judges would have to rank that grid more highly than the ones preferred by Frank and/or Peter. That's theoretically possible, I surmise, but a pretty thin pathway to walk. Better to just make sure I come up with an entry that's not in their databases.

My first try for a non-U Q-entry is QANTAS, the Australian airline. I'd bet my left leg—and my right one, too, actually—that it's in both Peter and Frank's databases, but it's still a cute entry. I reject the similar QANDAS (that's Q&A's, as in "question and answer sessions"). QANDA is a common enough crossword entry, but the plural of it is slightly undesirable, plural nouns being very slightly worse crossword entries than singular nouns, all else being equal.

The non-Q letters in QANTAS are all common, and after a few minutes I come up with a decent fill:

GRID A

Nothing real obscure in here, but not using the full surname of artist Andrea del SARTO is a little inelegant, and
SEAR IN, which I planned to clue as "congeal, as a steak's
juices" isn't great. I label this "grid A" and set out to improve.

My next thought is to take a stab at cruciverbal greatness.
Why not? I insert the entry QWERTY down from the Q and go
to work. QWERTY, as in the keyboard, is a great entry. Again,
though, I'm haunted by the knowledge that it's almost certainly
in both databases I'm competing against, so any grid I find is
likely to already have been found by the comps, assuming
they've got all the other words in it, too. Is it possible that two or
more of the four competitors could wind up with the exact
same 5 x 6 grid? I suppose so, though it's not terribly likely,
and the moral victory would go to the comp in such a situation,
since it's likely to have whipped up the same grid in thirty seconds that took the human an hour or two to devise.

My QWERTY try goes nowhere. Unlike the last five letters in QANTAS, WERTY has some medium-to-high
scoring Scrabble letters in the W and the Y, and they're both
awkwardly placed. I can't make it work.

Next, I try following one of the theoretical ways of winning Byron and I had discussed beforehand. I had recently interviewed both Peter and Frank about their databases and had seen both in action, and got a demonstration about how their computers decided what to include and exclude from grids. And I found a possible Achilles' heel that could lead to a human victory: both databases choose only words for a given fill based on the minimum level of accepted entry. As I e-mailed Byron:

> I know that Peter and Frank's databases both pretty much exclude words valued under a certain level—both of them have ranked the entries in their databases on scales . . . Peter usually sets his comp to exclude words ranked 40 or below, which is a weakness. For example, say there's a 4 x 4 corner where what we'll call "Fill A" gives you eight words that rank 45, 50, 60, 60, 70, 70, 75, and 85. And there's a hypothetical "Fill B" whose eight words would rank 30, 50, 70, 80, 80, 85, 90, and 90. Peter's computer would choose Fill A even though Fill B has the higher average entry value, simply b/c it doesn't allow itself to use that 30 word. So this is one area where we might be able to reign supreme— really going for it in corners where one or two weak entries allow us to use five or six really good entries.

Maybe, I reasoned, I could use one not-so-great word that's

value in their databases is below the minimum threshold, so it won't get picked. But that less-than-great word might allow a handful of excellent entries into the grid, and that handful could sway the judges.

It sounded a little theoretical until I hit upon this grid, where the strategy materialized:

The iffy word is ALOUS, which refers to the baseball-playing family of Jesus, Felipe, and Matty Alou. They mostly played in the 1960s and '70s, but were pretty well-known then, and a fourth member of the family, Felipe's son Moises, has been a star player in the 1980s and '90s (and even today). But pluralizing a name is almost always viewed as sub-optimal; in this case, at least, there really is more than one well-known ALOU. It's legal to pluralize a name like OPRAH or UMA, where there's exactly one famous example, and clue it something like "Winfrey and name-sakes," but it's seriously frowned upon.

So ALOUS isn't a great entry, but it does allow some great things in there: QUAKER is a good word, with a nice, high-value K, and SON OF A, clued as "Swearing phrase" is a terrific entry, since a lot of people do just say "Son of a . . . ," allowing the listener to provide the offending noun of his choice. USHERS, STARS, EVOKE, and DEFER are all solid English words, and OLIVET is a well-known Biblical reference (plus Carolyn McCormick's character on *Law & Order*, Dr. Elizabeth Olivet.). DINAH is likewise good.

The only one I'm not pleased with is MADE D'S. It keeps this from being a fill I'm really, truly happy with. My clue would've been "Got bad grades," but a Google search on "got a D in math" (511 hits) and "made a D in math" (47 hits) convinces me that most people "get" grades instead of "making them." I curse the illogic of that, since you really do "make" your grades depending on how hard you work, don't you? Why should it be a passive verb? But anyway, there it is. As much as I like the grid, I've got to toss it aside. It's a real shame, too—MADE D'S wasn't likely to be in their databases, and SONOFA might have been new, too. It would've been a tough grid to beat. I play around a little with it, hoping for a miracle fix, but there's nothing in sight— with a 5 x 6 grid, it's very tough to just change one or two letters and still have everything work. It's just too wide open, and too easy for the balancing act to collapse in ruin.

Following on the trail of SON OF A, I decide to try to come up with a different entry that won't be in the databases. Scanning the down entries, my mind suddenly comes upon OLA RAY, a six-letter entry down from the O.

Let me spoil the ending here: I wind up using OLA RAY, and it winds up backfiring horrifically. If at this point you're asking yourself "What on earth is OLA RAY?" then you're not alone. Four of the five judges, when they hand back their rankings to me, specifically cite it as a weak entry. "OLA RAY is pretty damn obscure," one judge writes. "I know her, but I suspect not one solver in 10,000 would." Another judge writes simply: "Ick."

I guess I'd better tell you who OLA RAY is now, assuming you're not one of the 1 in 10,000 people who already knows: she's an actress whose most famous role was co-starring with Michael Jackson in the "Thriller" video. I was ten years old when it came out in 1982, and it's arguably the most famous music video of all time, so I thought it was a peachy entry, in a trivia-ish kind of way, but the judges strongly disagreed. Here was my final grid:

M	O	S	Q	U
A	L	T	U	S
S	A	R	A	H
A	R	I	S	E
D	A	K	A	R
A	Y	E	R	S

I chose this over my other grids because I liked all the proper nouns, even though some of them are semi-tough: SARAH no one would have a problem with, but MASADA, ALTUS, AYERS, and DAKAR might be difficult. MASADA is the book/TV miniseries about the ancient revolt of the Jews in Judaea (and, of course, the fortress where it took place); ALTUS is an Air Force base in Oklahoma; and

AYERS is Australia's Ayers Rock, a big tourist attraction.
DAKAR is Senegal's capital.

When the grids came in from the other three contestants,
I scanned them over.

Here is the other humanoid grid, Byron Walden's:

M	O	S	Q	U
T	H	E	U	N
O	T	R	A	S
S	H	E	R	E
S	A	N	T	A
A	T	E	S	T

And now, the two computer grids. First, Frank Longo's:

M	O	S	Q	U
T	H	E	U	N
S	Y	N	O	D
N	E	A	T	O
O	A	T	E	N
W	H	E	R	E

And finally, Peter Gordon's:

M	O	S	Q	U
I	M	O	U	T
N	E	N	E	H
E	L	I	Z	A
R	E	C	O	N
S	T	E	N	T

Which of these four grids do you like best? I was, to be honest, somewhat underwhelmed when I saw the other three guys'. In Peter's grid, I liked I'M OUT, ELIZA, RECON, U THANT (former Secretary General of the U.N.), and SO NICE. OMELET, MINERS, and STENT are all fine, and I like QUEZON (as in Quezon City, former capital of the Philippines). But NENEH (as in singer Neneh Cherry) surprised me, since I thought she was just a 1980s one-hit wonder (though I found out later that she's got some indie music street cred in addition to her major pop hit, the catchy "Buffalo Stance").

OTRAS (Spanish for "others") and A TEST (short for "Atomic test," i.e. the testing of an atomic bomb) weren't great in Byron's grid, though I did like MT. OSSA, OH THAT, and THE U.N.

Frank's grid really surprised me, though. I had never heard of MT. SNOW, and OATEN and QUOTER were weak, I felt. THE U.N. (same word and same place as in Byron's grid, interestingly) was good, and OH YEAH was very good, and the other words were all good dictionary entries. But I felt that the weakness of MT. SNOW, OATEN, and QUOTER were near-fatal.

Shows what I know: when the judges returned their scores, Frank's grid had four first place finishes and one second place finish. I'd asked the judges to rank each of the four entries by overall quality, however they defined it. A first place finish got four points, a second place three points, third place two points, and fourth place one point. Based on this system, Frank Longo's 5 x 6 grid earned an amazing 19 points from a possible 20. Peter Gordon was second, having snatched away one first-place vote from Frank, with 13 points total. Byron Walden was third with 11 points, and I was a miserable last place with 7 (four last place finishes and one second place).

Judges loved Longo's grid ("easily the best of the lot," said one), citing THE U.N. and OH YEAH as star entries. It turns out that MT. SNOW is a you-know-it-or-you-don't entry, two of the judges having specifically referenced it as good, and two others having never heard of it.

Gordon's grid did well, too, the Z getting praise from all corners (Gordon was the only competitor to work another of the four rare letters into the 5 x 6 grid besides the already present Q). He had to pay a price to get it in, however, as often happens with a rare letter: three of the five judges cited NENEH/QUEZON as a difficult crossing (which I didn't agree with, but they're the judges).

Walden's grid got praise for MT. OSSA, but drew unexpected fire for OH THAT, which was, in my view a strong entry.

So the 5 x 6 task produced a clear winner in Frank Longo, and a clear victory for the computer-aided grids over the humans, 32 points to 18. Accuse me of sour grapes if you must, but I didn't find this victory very conclusive; since all four constructors produced several finished grids but could choose only one, it came down to as much of an editorial decision as it was a test of constructing skill. Perhaps if I'd chosen a non-OLA RAY grid, the humans might have done better, or even won. And the same might be said of the other constructors; Gordon, for example, might have reconsidered his QUEZON/NENEH crossing if he'd known three of the five judges would cite it as too tough, and picked another grid instead.

The 5 x 6 task went to the comps, then, but I couldn't help thinking that that particular task I'd set had been interesting but perhaps not entirely relevant. It was too small a canvas to judge accurately, something like running a ten-yard dash to determine who the fastest runner is. We hadn't truly gotten at the core issue, I felt, which is whether a human or a computer can build a better crossword grid. For that we would have to turn to the second task, the actual crossword grid itself: the 15 x 15s. This would be the hundred-yard dash, and no sour grapes if the humans lost.

Life lesson learned working at a summer camp: there was a counselor whose strategy for winning daily cleanliness awards at cabin inspection was to overwhelm the judge with a brilliant first impression. He instructed his campers to use so many aromatic cleaning sprays that right when the judge stepped in the cabin, he'd be amazed at how nice it smelled, and that positive first thought would outlast any flaws found upon closer inspection.

This was going to be my strategy for the 15 x 15 grid, too. I wanted so many X's and Q's and J's and Z's in that grid that they'd catch those judges' eyes first thing, and hold so tight that they wouldn't notice the crosswordese that'd crept in to accommodate those high-value letters.

This meant, of course, oodles of these: beyond the three pre-placed ones in the grid (the X in BOXLEITNER, the Z in BEREZOVSKY, and the J in BENJAMIN), my final grid contained six other rare letters, more than either of the computer-aided grids did (Longo had none, Gordon had four). Walden apparently worked at summer camp, too, since his grid likewise contained six additional rare letters.

But, as often happens with rare letters, I paid a price for it: my grid also had lousy entries like ATO ("From ___ Z," a legit-but-dull crossword standard), EEEEE ("Widest male shoe size") and INE ("Chemistry suffix") scattered around it. True, there were some really nice entries, like THX (short for "thanks") and ZZ TOP and ZUCCHINI and SHORT I'S ("Some vowels"), but overall it was a grid with lots of pluses and lots of minuses. I was hoping the pluses would put the judges into my corner.

My final entry:

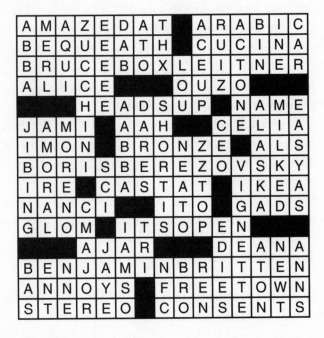

A	M	A	Z	E	D	A	T		A	R	A	B	I	C
B	E	Q	U	E	A	T	H		C	U	C	I	N	A
B	R	U	C	E	B	O	X	L	E	I	T	N	E	R
A	L	I	C	E			O	U	Z	O				
		H	E	A	D	S	U	P		N	A	M	E	
J	A	M	I		A	A	H		C	E	L	I	A	
I	M	O	N		B	R	O	N	Z	E		A	L	S
B	O	R	I	S	B	E	R	E	Z	O	V	S	K	Y
I	R	E		C	A	S	T	A	T		I	K	E	A
N	A	N	C	I			I	T	O		G	A	D	S
G	L	O	M		I	T	S	O	P	E	N			
		A	J	A	R				D	E	A	N	A	
B	E	N	J	A	M	I	N	B	R	I	T	T	E	N
A	N	N	O	Y	S		F	R	E	E	T	O	W	N
S	T	E	R	E	O		C	O	N	S	E	N	T	S

Byron Walden's:

A	B	B	E		L	E	P	E	W		A	B	I	T
M	A	R	X		I	R	A	N	I		R	E	N	O
B	R	U	C	E	B	O	X	L	E	I	T	N	E	R
I	N	T	U	X	E	D	O	S		D	I	Z	Z	Y
		S	I	R	E	S		L	I	C				
A	L	W	E	S	T		B	I	G	L	I	A	R	
L	E	I		T	Y	P	E	I	N		E	T	N	A
B	O	R	I	S	B	E	R	E	Z	O	V	S	K	Y
O	X	E	N		O	P	E	N	E	R		U	L	E
M	I	D	J	U	N	E		R	S	V	P	E	D	
		U	N	D		S	A	T	I	E				
B	R	O	N	C		L	E	M	O	N	S	O	L	E
B	E	N	J	A	M	I	N	B	R	I	T	T	E	N
L	E	T	O		O	N	S	E	T		R	O	A	D
S	L	O	E		D	E	E	R	E		Y	E	N	S

Frank Longo's:

D	A	N	M	A	R	I	N	O		D	A	N	T	E
A	R	E	A	C	O	D	E	S		A	L	O	H	A
B	R	U	C	E	B	O	X	L	E	I	T	N	E	R
B	I	T	E				T	O	G	S		U	S	C
E	V	E	R	A	G	E			G	E	I	S	H	A
D	E	R		L	A	U	D	E		S	H	E	E	N
		W	A	R	G	A	M	E		A	R	I	D	
B	O	R	I	S	B	E	R	E	Z	O	V	S	K	Y
A	V	I	D		O	N	E	T	I	M	E			
D	E	D	E	E		E	D	I	N	A		M	L	B
D	R	E	N	C	H		C	E	N	T	A	U	R	
E	L	I		L	E	G	G			I	N	C	A	
B	E	N	J	A	M	I	N	B	R	I	T	T	E	N
T	A	T	E	S		R	A	T	I	S	L	A	N	D
S	P	O	T	S		D	R	U	G	T	E	S	T	S

And Peter Gordon's:

J	O	P	L	I	N		C	R	A	S	H	P	A	D
O	T	O	O	L	E		C	U	T	L	O	O	S	E
B	R	U	C	E	B	O	X	L	E	I	T	N	E	R
S	A	R	A	N		C	L	E	A	N		D	A	N
	B	L	E	S	T			M	G	M				
Z	O	O	S		C	O	A	L	S		A	D	I	N
U	Z	I		S	A	B	R	E		B	R	A	N	S
B	O	R	I	S	B	E	R	E	Z	O	V	S	K	Y
I	N	E	P	T		R	A	J	A	S		K	E	N
N	E	S	S		P	S	Y	C	H		M	A	R	C
		O	B	I		O	N	T	A	P				
E	M	O		R	E	H	A	B		A	R	I	S	E
B	E	N	J	A	M	I	N	B	R	I	T	T	E	N
R	A	C	E	C	A	R	D		E	N	H	A	L	O
O	D	D	M	E	N	T	S		S	T	A	L	L	S

The data points were a lot more scattershot for this task than for the 5 x 6; each of the four participants got at least one last place vote, since I was generous and didn't hog them this time, and three of the four contestants (all but Longo) got at least one first-place vote. Most amazingly, two of the judges ranked the four grids in the precise reverse order of each other!

In the end, Byron's grid prevailed with 14 points, a moral victory for humanity. Close behind were Peter and Frank with 13 each, and I brought up the caboose (again, sigh) with 10 points.

In Byron's winning entry, judges liked INJUN JOE, LEMON SOLE, I DIG, and ARTICLE V. IN TUXEDOS was slammed as a contrived phrase, but it didn't keep the puzzle from taking two of the five first-place votes.

In Frank's grid, judges liked DAN MARINO, EAR CANDY, and EZINE, but weren't partial to RAT ISLAND, which was deemed a little obscure.

Peter's grid got official props for LEE J. COBB, N SYNC, and CRASH PAD, but POURBOIRES, a French word meaning "tips," as in a restaurant or bar, was cited by two judges as being outside their ken. Subjectivity again: Gordon included it on purpose, because he thought it was an especially good entry.

My grid drew both the praise and condemnation I expected: one first-place vote but two last place votes as well (one judge wrote: "This puzzle, to me, screams 'trying too hard' ").

Final score for the 15 x 15s: Computers 26, Humans 24.

Overall total score: Computer 58, Humans 42. I tip my hat to our cyberchampions, but will not hesitate to unplug them if they get too smug in victory.

Naturally no one small sample test proves anything with certainty, and, unlike with the cold results of a chess match, there's enough subjectivity and other noise in crossword puzzle judging that humans will be able to hang around for a long time. Different competitors, different judges, a different day: anything could've pushed the results one way or the other. But I promised no sour grapes, so I'll shut up now. The computers won this battle, and that's that. Grrr.

Will I be jumping on board the database ship? It may be a poor career move, but I will not. As a natural contrarian, I'd rather spend my time figuring out ways to win a rematch than join the other team. If you check back in ten years, though, the progress computers have made might finally have pushed me over the edge, in which case I can always fall back on making a living at another hobby of mine, chess—except that Deep Blue might have something to say there as well.

CHAPTER 7

From A to Banzai

Have you ever wanted to sit at a crossword constructor's elbow while he writes, just to sneak a look at the puzzle-making process? To observe him brainstorming and honing a theme; to study him carefully plotting the grid and crafting the clues; to sucker punch him in the back of the neck for all those years of torment?

You've come to the right place, then, minus the sucker punch thing (don't try it; I've got the reflexes of a veldt-hardened wildebeest). In this chapter I'm going to write a daily-size crossword from start to finish, and you're free to observe the whole thing—the false starts, the imperfections, the lucky breaks—everything that takes place along the minor journey of writing a puzzle. And it is a journey; a key part of the experience is going along to wherever the cross-word gods have determined the letters will take you.

A crossword begins with a theme. Like they say love does, the theme for this puzzle comes to me from out of nowhere when I'm not looking for it. About half the themes I use find me in this manner instead of the other way around.

In this particular case I am gathering some papers up around my desk, and my eye chances upon the words ARE and EAR crossing in a puzzle grid. The theme antennae of the crossword writer are always on low-level alert, and finely tuned to picking up ideas from the language we hear and see around us. Like a city rat that thinks he smells lunch in the trash can down the alley, the crossword constructor is happy to follow a promising trail for a block or two in hopes of finding something worthwhile. If it shakes out, you've got a theme; if it doesn't, you forget it and go back about your life, keeping your whiskers primed for the next lead.

Here my whiskers notice that ARE and EAR are anagrams of each other, and that their reversals, ERA and RAE, are also cluable crossword entries (RAE could refer to the actresses Rae Dawn Chong and Charlotte Rae).

Walking down the alley a bit, I realize that the only other two permutations of those three letters, AER and REA, are also cluable, making all six possible combinations of these three letters legit crossword entries (AER Lingus is Ireland's national carrier, and a frequent puzzle guest—you might call it the official airline of the crossword community).

Cool, I think, but how unusual is this? If it turns out to be a common phenomenon, then it's probably not a real special theme. If, say, two dozen three-letter combinations yield six cluable entries apiece, then it's like having "Countries that Start with A" as your theme—big whoop, there's a million of 'em.

But I soon realize that this A-R-E is a special series. Running through the possibilities for a few minutes, I am unable to come up with any other three-letter combinations that work. There are a couple of close tries: T-S-E yields TSE ("Mao ___-tung," among other clues), SET, STE ("Sault ___ Marie, Mich."), EST ("Superlative ending"), ETS (a borderline but often seen entry, clued along the lines of "Spielbergian creatures"), but then TES is a problem. Might be cluable in some obscure way, but I don't know how. At any rate, the A-R-E set begins to look more and more like a unique and themeworthy grouping.

My first thought is: how about six phrases that include one of these six words each in them? If I can get the letters to work right, this will be a nice, tight little theme, and jamming six theme entries into a 15 x 15 grid would be a robust challenge indeed, so let's see how it pans out.

The first one of the six I begin with is AER LINGUS, because my possibilities for using AER in a phrase are pretty much limited to that one option. There is an Irish regional airline called Aer Arann, which you'll occasionally see from a constructor looking for a break from the "___ Lingus (Irish airline)" standby, but it's still not well-known enough to use as a theme entry. So I mark a "9" by AER LINGUS, since it's nine letters long, and focus on which entries are next most restricted in their options of phrase.

The next two candidates look like RAE and REA. ARE has a million possibilities, like YOU ARE HERE or ARE YOU JOKING or WE ARE THE WORLD and so forth. EAR is similarly bountiful, yielding PLAY IT BY EAR, BEND SOMEONE'S EAR, EAR OF CORN, etc. ERA is just as easy: BIG BAND ERA, COMPUTER ERA, PALEO-ZOIC ERA, and many more.

With REA and RAE, however, I can only think of two

phrases each that are well-known enough: the actor STEPHEN REA and comic/actress CAROLINE REA, plus the actresses CHARLOTTE RAE and RAE DAWN CHONG (lots of thespians around these parts; the movie *Norma Rae*, incidentally, would be too short to work as a theme entry). For the RAE actresses, I'm sure enough about their names to not look them up, but I'm only about 98 percent sure that it's "Stephen" Rea and not "Steven," so I hop on over to the Internet Movie Database to double check. I'm also about 95 percent sure that Caroline Rea was the star of the sitcom *Caroline in the City*, which I never watched, but which was on my cultural radar nonetheless due to its recent popularity.

Statistically speaking, there's a 100 percent chance that I'm going to check on the theme entries I'm 98 percent and 95 percent sure of. I had a few experiences early in my puzzle-writing career of constructing an entire crossword only to realize I had a big, honkin', unchangeable theme entry misspelled smack dab in the center of the grid. From this I learned to check on the 95- and 98-percenters. It's like discovering that the main beam holding up your house was made with a rotten log; there's nothing to do but tear down and start over again.

My best example of this was QUETZALCOATL in a puzzle for *Dell Champion* in the late 1980s, where the theme was words with both a Q and a Z. I had misspelled the Aztec god's name as QUETZACOATL, which I suppose counts as sacrilege from a religious viewpoint. It was definitely a crossword sin; the editor wrote me a nasty note when returning the grid, since she hadn't spotted it herself until she'd already wasted an hour on the puzzle.

In this case due diligence pays off: the 98 percent Stephen

Rea checks out OK, but Lea Thompson was the star of Caroline in the City, not Caroline Rea. Not fatal, but utterly fatal is that the comic/actress I'm thinking of isn't "Caroline Rea," but "Rhea." Rotten log avoided; STEPHEN REA it is, and I mark a "10" by his name.

The reason I'm marking the lengths of the theme entries is that each one needs a twin, the symmetry and rules of crosswords demanding a nine-letter entry, for example, to offset AER LINGUS in the grid. The only exception to this would be a theme entry running across the middle of the grid, which needs no counterpart; but with an even number of theme entries in this puzzle, we won't have that.

Slight disappointment comes when I count out the lengths for CHARLOTTE RAE and RAE DAWN CHONG, as both come in at twelve letters long. I'd prefer they be differing lengths to give me more flexibility in the other theme possibilities, but you can't have everything in life. Besides, there are so many good choices with ARE, EAR, and ERA that I don't think there'll be much problem at all finding buddies for AER, REA, and RAE, so I mark a "12" next to RAE and move along.

We've got a 9, 10, and 12 to offset with these last three, and the two REAs actually do give me a little flexibility in another area of finishing off this theme. Here's how: when you have a theme comprised of entries with something in common, you don't want the common threads to be placed differently in one theme entry than in the others. For example, if your theme were phrases containing royal flush cards, your theme would be humming along fine with PERFECT TEN, PANAMA JACK, GOD SAVE THE QUEEN,

and RODNEY KING, but would stall once you hit ACE
VENTURA. The card is used as the last word in all the
entries but that one, which makes it stick out too much;
this inelegance alone would get the puzzle clipped by most
editors.

In order to get around that, you'd have to come up with a
ten-letter phrase (to offset PERFECT TEN) that ended in the
word ACE. Since there isn't such a phrase (that I can think of,
anyway) you could escape in the other direction: just change
PANAMA JACK to JACK LONDON, meaning two of the five
theme entries start with the face card, while three end with it.
That's enough of a mix to make editors happy; though they
might slightly prefer to have all five be similarly placed, no
editor is likely to reject this theme on that basis.

Which leads us back to our theme: as I'm coming up with
the last three entries for it, I've got to make sure I don't get
stuck with an orphan like ACE VENTURA in the example
above. This is the flexibility I mentioned that the two RAE
actresses permits, a flexibility which ensures my theme
won't meet this fate: if I need another phrase where the A-
R-E anagram is at the beginning, I can use RAE DAWN
CHONG, while if I need one where it appears at the end, I
can use CHARLOTTE RAE. This duo is the type O blood of
theme entries—they'll work with just about anybody, and
I'm glad to have these team players on board.

With this freedom in mind, I quickly come up with WHO
ARE YOU, CLINTON ERA, and PLAYS IT BY EAR as
nine-, ten-, and twelve-letter entries to offset my other three.
No orphans, either: AER LINGUS and RAE DAWN
CHONG (she balances things better here than Charlotte, as

it turns out) both begin with the anagram; PLAYS IT BY EAR, CLINTON ERA, and STEPHEN REA end with it; and WHO ARE YOU has it right in the center, which is a nice mixer-upper as well. Especially with six theme entries in a 15 x 15 grid, which is a lot, editors won't mind that the anagram isn't in the same place in all six entries just as long, as is the case here, that five aren't one way and the sixth entry another.

I Google "Clinton Era" as a paranoid check—never hurts—and it comes back with 600,000-plus hits, so I'm ready to roll. A crossword puzzle theme has been birthed!

Before we move on to the next step, filling the grid, I pause to wonder for a moment if this theme has ever been done before. I suspect that it has, since most themes have, and this is a cute but not particularly hidden idea for a puzzle theme.

If another constructor has done it before, or if one does it in the future, the odds are good that their puzzle is going to look very much like mine. It's shocking the first time you see a theme of yours anticipated (or followed) by another constructor, since many or perhaps all of your theme entries are in their grid, too; it looks like one of you just copied from the other.

But this is virtually never the case, since the cruciverbal crowd is pretty much an honest crowd. Instead, consider how likely it is that a constructor who comes upon the six-different-anagrams-of-the-three-letter-word idea would follow my path almost precisely. First, I've already determined that A-R-E is the only valid triad of letters where all six anagram into something useful. Ergo, that hypothetical other constructor would have to use my same letters if he wanted to use this theme at all. AER LINGUS, STEPHEN REA, and one of my twelve-letter RAEs they'd also be forced to use, and PLAYS IT BY EAR is the commonest of the happy EAR choices, so they'd likely use that one as well. They might choose something like SILENT ERA as the nine and ARE YOU SURE for the ten, or some other minor alternative to my last two. But when they're all done, their puzzle is likely to have three or four of its six theme entries identical to mine.

The first time this happened I thought I'd caught a plagiarist, but then I realized how truly narrow the path can be through a particular jungle of wordplay, and I wasn't surprised the next time someone else showed up at my campsite in the middle of the rain forest.

On to the fill. The first step is to place the theme entries in the grid; the number and lengths of the entries will play a big part in determining where they go. For three fifteen-letter entries, as in the humans vs. computers battle in the previous chapter, the answer is obvious: the three grid-spanning theme words would almost always go directly across the grid in the third, eighth, and thirteenth rows. For three fifteens, it's the most logical placing by far.

For six theme entries of varying lengths as we've got here, there's more room for creativity—and trouble, too, since six theme entries is on the high end for 15 x 15 puzzles.

When deciding where to place the theme words, I have to keep in mind the main rules of constructing: the grid must have 180-degree rotational symmetry, contain no words shorter than three letters in length, and each letter in the grid must be part of both an across and a down word.

Besides paying attention to these restrictions, I've got to make sure the letters in the theme words don't bump up against each other in unpleasant ways. For instance, while first playing around with this theme, I tried to stack the theme entries like so:

This would have left me with some problems, however. The central area looks tough to fill, with four theme entries zipping through it, but I don't even try to do so, since I spot a couple of dealbreakers right off the bat: for the symmetrically-placed down entries D _ P _ L and E _ G _ Y, I can't think of a word that fits either pattern.

Once I hit a rock wall like this, I've got to either futz with the pattern of black squares, or try swapping a few of the same-length theme entries for each other, or, if all else fails, clear the grid and start over from scratch (easier to do when working with Crossword Compiler, as I do now, than when working with graph paper and pencil, as I used to).

After a few more tries, I finally get what looks like a placement of theme entries I can work with.

A quick scan of the grid doesn't reveal any areas that look impossible to fill, so I get to work. During the fill, I'm always on the lookout to squeeze rare letters into the mix if I can, but with so many theme entries flying around this puzzle it's going to be tough. Maybe I'll be able to slip an X into a circumscribed little corner somewhere, like the upper right or lower right, but the middle section of the grid probably isn't going to see any rare letter action. I'll be happy enough just to get a decent fill in there, so a high-value letter looks like a long shot.

But long shots sometimes go in, and here I score bigtime in the lower-central section of the grid, where UZI crosses the Japanese war yell BANZAI. Excellent—if there's any way I can keep that Z I'm going to, since I'm a sucker for pricy letters.

Up top, I wind up having to change CLINTON ERA to FLAPPER ERA—not a bust on the ex-president (who's a big crossword fan, incidentally), but the T in CLINTON wasn't working well with the O and L in CHONG and LINGUS (there's a sex joke in this paragraph someplace, but I can't find it).

It's not unusual to change a theme entry like this as the grid progresses. In a previous incarnation of the fill, I'd tried JACKSON ERA, KENNEDY ERA, and BIG BAND ERA before changing it to FLAPPER ERA. It's all part of the going-where-the-puzzle-leads-you art of crossword writing.

Finally I've got what looks like a decent fill. Judge for yourself:

G	I	G	S	■	E	P	S	O	M	■	A	T	A	D
O	S	L	O	■	L	O	O	P	Y	■	R	I	C	E
F	O	O	L	■	F	L	A	P	P	E	R	E	R	A
A	L	B	I	N	O	■	■	E	R	O	D	E	D	■
R	A	E	D	A	W	N	C	H	O	N	G	■	■	■
■	■	■	S	L	I	D	U	P	■	A	I	D	E	■
B	A	I	L	S	■	A	E	R	L	I	N	G	U	S
A	G	R	E	E	D	■	■	E	M	C	E	E	S	■
W	H	O	A	R	E	Y	O	U	■	B	E	R	L	E
L	A	N	D	■	B	A	N	Z	A	I	■	■	■	■
■	P	L	A	Y	S	I	T	B	Y	E	A	R	■	■
L	A	R	I	A	T	■	■	L	E	A	N	T	O	■
S	T	E	P	H	E	N	R	E	A	■	C	L	A	W
A	R	I	E	■	R	O	O	K	S	■	H	A	L	E
T	A	N	S	■	S	W	E	E	T	■	T	I	L	L

There's some good stuff in here, like GO FAR, MY PEOPLE, SLID UP, YACHT, YAY, and ELF OWL (the smallest variety of owl; a semi-tough word, but it's intuitively guessable with a clue hinting at a small bird, so not a big deal).

I make a list of all "problem entries" to see how clean the fill is. Some problem entries aren't really problems at all: abbreviations, partials and the like are totally legit words, but the kind you want to keep to a minimum. My list of words that are in some way less than perfect comes to eleven: LSAT, ISOLA, AGHA, LAH, SOA, CDE, ONS,

HUR, OPP, ERN, and ESSE. Everything else in the grid is either OK or better than OK, so let's look at the problem children one at a time.

LSAT is only on the list because it's an abbreviation. It's a common one, though, so not actually a real problem at all, especially since there are only two abbreviations in the entire grid.

ISOLA, the Italian word for "island," is next. Not a real commonly known foreign word, but it's close to the English, and no difficult words cross it, so it goes into the acceptable folder as well.

AGHA is the alternative spelling of the Turkish title AGA. Not beautiful, but again, no tough words cross it, so we'll let it slide, though I'm not entirely happy about it.

LAH is a partial, to be clued as "___-di-dah (pretentious)." Partials are rarely elegant, but there are only three in this grid, so that's fine.

SO A is another of the three partials. I'll Google a quotation later to clue that one.

CDE is easy to clue as "Alphabetical sequence" or, "B followers" if I want to get a little tricky. It probably shouldn't even be on the problem list, since such alphabetical sequences are common in puzzles.

ONS is also easy to clue as "Come-___ (marketing techniques)" or "Light switch settings." Again, not a real problem.

HUR is "Ben-___," again only on the list because it's a partial.

OPP is the second abbreviation in the grid, short for "opponent."

ERN isn't a great entry, but a regular puzzle guest clued as "Ending for north or south" or "Directional suffix."

Finally, ESSE is Latin for "to be." Pretty well-known as far as Latin words go.

All in all, a fairly clean fill for a 15 x 15 with six theme entries running through it. A few abbreviations, a few partials, a couple of toughish foreign words, but no major blots, and no prohibitively difficult crossings. If this baby were messier I'd try to massage a few of the problem entries out. But the grid's good as is, and I don't see an easy way to work even ISOLA out (I take a few minutes' stab at it, but don't come up with anything better, especially since I like all the fill words in that corner besides ISOLA).

That's that; let's call it a grid and move on to the clues.

Based on the difficulty level of the theme entries I decide this is going to be about a Wednesday-level puzzle, and clue accordingly. Just a few gimmes, like "Wore away" for ERODED and "Hamilton died in one" for DUEL. Then a thick layer of medium-difficulty clues, like "Plot of land, sometimes" for ACRE and "Spinnable sphere" for GLOBE. Finally, three or four tough clues, like "Roughly one out of every 17,000 people" for ALBINO and "Point makers" for DEBATERS. These tough clues are like putting a drop of Tabasco sauce in a big bowl of stew; it'll make the whole thing just a little sharper in taste, and you don't need much of it.

Finally it's time to edit. I fact-check the various clues, looking up anything I'm not 99.9 percent sure of. In this case, I had to look up (among other entries) acting credits for the NIA Peeples clue, make sure Robert IGER is still CEO of Disney, and confirm that the 1920s was roughly the FLAPPER ERA.

Now the final task: the title. A crossword's title should in some way point to the theme's gimmick, but not be so obvious that it gives the trick away before the solver even begins. Ideally, about halfway through the solve, there'll be an "oh, now I get it" moment.

I brainstorm title ideas for this puzzle: "Three of a Kind" isn't snappy enough. "Triple Play" is closer, but a set of three letters isn't really a "triple," so that's not perfect. How about something with "trio," since it's a trio of letters that does all the moving and shaking in this theme?

"Trio Riot" springs to mind, and I like it. It has the word *trio,* implying a group of three; the two words in it are anagrams of each other, hinting there'll be a little shuffling of letters going on; and "riot" can imply either that it's a lot of fun (as in "that guy's a riot") or just imply general wackiness, which fits, too. So "Trio Riot" is our winner.

And that's our crossword! If I had an editor for this puzzle, I'd e-mail it off now and feel pretty confident about receiving a yes.

Turn the page to see the finished product. Elapsed time, from concept to fruition: five hours, twenty-seven minutes.

TRIO RIOT

ACROSS

1 Short-term jobs
5 ___ salts
10 Sort of
14 Cold capital
15 Nuts
16 Staple in Singapore
17 Pull a fast one on
18 The 1920s, roughly
20 Roughly one out of every 17,000 people
22 Wore away
23 *Soul Man* actress
27 Climbed stealthily
28 Assistant
32 Opts out of an activity
36 Irish carrier
38 "Ditto"
40 Runs the event
41 Sentinel's query
45 "Uncle Miltie"
46 Hit shore
47 Japanese war shout
49 Doesn't plan things in advance
55 Lasso
58 Adirondack structure
59 *The Crying Game* actor
63 Crab part
64 India.___ (noted singer)
65 Board figures

66 Looking healthy
67 Lays out
68 "That's awesome!"
69 Money drawer

DOWN

1 Have success
2 Island: It.
3 Spinnable sphere
4 Reliable
5 Smallest species of a certain bird
6 Dem. or Rep., casually
7 "___ day's journey in oblivious haze"—Keats
8 The other guy: abbr.
9 Emotional reference to an audience
10 Smug quality
11 1-1, say
12 Plot of land, sometimes
13 A goner
19 North or south ending
21 Former Egyptian leader
24 Peeples of *Walker, Texas Ranger*
25 B followers
26 *Ben-___*
29 Disney CEO Robert
30 Hamilton died in one
31 To be: Lat.
32 Cry like a baby

33 Turk's title: var.
34 Wood alternative
35 Water carriers?
37 Drink
39 Point makers
42 "Hurrah!"
43 Light switch settings
44 Gun from Israel
48 "Finally!"
50 ___-di-dah (pretentious)
51 Big boat

52 Chou ___
53 To any degree
54 Wheel on a spur
55 Test for future attys.
56 Razor brand
57 Get under control (with "in")
60 "This instant!"
61 Fish eggs
62 Squeeze (out)

CHAPTER 8

Themes, Grids, and Clues

In the 1920s, world chess champion Jose Raoul Capablanca complained that chess was "played out." The opening moves of the game had been studied so thoroughly, he argued, that it wasn't fun anymore. Players would regularly reel off their first fifteen or twenty moves without even thinking, since they had been played many times before. To inject new life into the game, Capa even proposed expanding the chessboard from 8 x 8 squares to 10 x 10.

A similar crisis exists today in the realm of crossword puzzles, and it involves crossword themes, which are something of a damsel in distress. The problem is straightforward: there isn't much left that hasn't been done before.

A crossword puzzle's theme is the unifying thread among several prominent entries in the grid, usually the longest entries. They've never been officially classified, but there are about a dozen broad categories of crossword theme. Though the occasional unique, totally original theme pops up from time to time, the vast majority of themed puzzles you come across will fall into one of these well-trodden categories.

First, the rarely seen nowadays, much-derided repeated word themes. These used to be popular back in the early days of themed puzzles, but now they're usually mocked as hackwork by puzzle snobs. They are indeed pretty simple: a keyword is repeated in each of the theme entries, like HOUSE in the phrases WHITE HOUSE, TOWNHOUSE, PLAYS HOUSE, and DOLLHOUSE. These don't show up often nowadays; in fact, most top editors specifically ban them.

Kicking it up a notch, we turn to the something-in-common themes. Just as it sounds, the theme entries share some feature, or are members of a certain group. Example: in a 2003 puzzle, Patrick Jordan used LEAVE IN THE LURCH, THE REAL THING, and ASH WEDNESDAY as theme phrases. The fourth entry, THE ADDAMS FAMILY, gave away what the other three had in common: each phrase contained a member of the adorably creepy TV clan.

Another standby is the pun theme. Merl Reagle once wrote a crossword whose theme was puns on philosophers' names (if you're eating something right now, consider putting it aside). He unleashed on solvers:

16-down: "A philosophy class lament about lost crib sheets?" Answer: WHERE ARE YOU NOW THAT I NIET-ZSCHE?

23-across: "Get a head start in philosophy class?" Answer: SCHOPENHAUER EARLY.

88-across: "Disparaging remark about a philosopher?" Answer: WHAT DOES ZENO?

110-across: "Students' complaint in philosophy class?" Answer: IT'LL JUST CONFUCIUS.

Then there are the drop/add/change something themes,

highly frequent puzzle page visitors. In order to get the correct theme answers, the solver has to drop or add a letter or letters from a phrase to leave a new phrase, or change the original phrase in some other way.

In a puzzle titled "Leave Me out of This!" the solver may have to remove the letters ME from phrases to get the theme entries. So "Where an astronomer sleeps?" would be HALLEY'S COT, while "Well-mannered guy on the 'M*A*S*H' set?" would yield GENTLEMAN FARR.

You may also have to add a letter (or letters) instead of removing them as in the above example, or replace some letters with certain other letters. In a puzzle called "Go for It," for instance, you may have to substitute the letters GO for the letters IT in the puzzle's the theme entries.

These drop/add/change themes are so common and their titles so often such giveaways that they're becoming a little passé these days. Once you've seen enough titles like "Doggone" (where you have to remove the letters DOG from theme answers) and "Plush" (where you have to add the letter H to them) they stop fooling you, and the themes are often easily guessable from the title alone.

Beyond these we have rebus themes, where a symbol or series of letters must be fit into certain theme entry squares; quotation themes, where a quote is chopped up and scattered around the grid for the solver to piece back together; and several other minor types in addition.

Although only a sliver of themes you'll run across won't fit into one of the known groupings, this isn't to say that there's nothing new out there at all. On occasion, a constructor will find a clever, *sui generis* theme that can never be repeated.

One 1994 puzzle by Wayne Robert Williams was called "Playing the Angles," and theme answers all indeed had something angular about them: UP AROUND THE BEND, CORNER THE MARKET, and so on. The clever trick was that several squares in the grid appeared divided by a backslash where theme entries crossed, and the answer itself actually turned there. So 15-across was the eleven-letter answer ELBOW GREASE, with the third square containing the backslash. Solvers had to fill in EL normally, then put the B in the lower-left half of the backslash-split square, then curve downward for eight squares to finish the answer vertically with OW GREASE.

Wonderful stuff, but such original ideas are getting harder and harder to find. And once a solver is familiar with a theme he is difficult to trick with it again.

My favorite theme of all time was an Eric Albert puzzle from the *New York Times* called "Night Lights." The puzzle appeared to be a standard rebus theme, with STAR as its keyword. This had been done a million times before, and while solving it, I was surprised that such a derivative theme would be used by such a skilled and creative constructor as Albert. Then I got to 68-across; I looked around the grid for a few seconds, took in vain the name of an historical figure many consider the Messiah, and knew this was the best crossword theme I'd ever seen.

The clue for 68-across was "What the lights in this puzzle form," and the answer was BIG DIPPER. When you connected the seven STARs Albert had strategically scattered in theme entries around the grid, they formed the familiar outline of that constellation.

Puzzles like this have what are sometimes termed "meta-themes"—at some point you have to step back from the puzzle and look at the grid as a whole to get the trick. Another meta-theme is my personal favorite from my own scrapbook.

The puzzle was called "Hidings," and appeared in the *Washington Post Magazine* in 1997. It looked like a regular crossword, albeit with a somewhat unusual pattern of black squares snaking around the center of the grid. As the solver progressed through the puzzle, the theme entries, clued as "Part 1 of instructions to the solver," "Part 2 of instructions," and so on, spelled out: "THE NINETEENTH LETTER OF THE ALPHABET CAN BE FOUND ONLY ONE PLACE IN THE ENTIRE PUZZLE GRID. TRY TO FIND IT."

But when the solver finished filling in the puzzle, there were no S's to be found (not an easy task to pull off, since S is naturally a very common crossword letter).

It was only when the solver turned the puzzle ninety degrees that he found the puzzle's lone S, formed by that unusual arrangement of black squares in the center of the grid.

Cool idea at the time, but even the notion of patterning the black squares in a significant way has been done repeatedly by now. In fact, it'd been done long before my puzzle arrived on the scene: in a self-tribute to his own initials, Henry Hook wrote a puzzle in the 1980s in which the central pattern of black squares formed a huge H. And it had probably been done before that, too.

What to do about the relative dearth of original themes? One answer is to simply make crosswords themeless, as they were during the first four decades of their existence (the first theme didn't pop up in a puzzle until the 1950s). Many puzzles already are, such as the Friday and Saturday *New York Times* crosswords, and those in increasing numbers of crossword books.

Without the constraint of theme entries to work around, constructors have freer rein to dive right in with juicy vocabulary like JOE MILLIONAIRE or EXIT WOUND. The vocabulary in themeless puzzles is often markedly fresher than in themed puzzles, for several reasons. In a themed puzzle, dozens of letters are placed in the grid before the fill is begun, severely limiting what the fill can contain. Also, fill words in themed puzzles tend to be three, four, five, and six letters in length, since the long theme entries require delicate footwork to accommodate, and shorter words work better for this—but there aren't many short words left that solvers haven't seen a hundred times already. A themeless 15 x 15 puzzle, on the other hand, will usually include a rich stock of seven-, eight-, nine-, and ten-letter words, which allows a much wider range of vocabulary, including more multi-word phrases, which tend to be fun (YOU BETCHA, GIMME THAT, WHAT'S NEW?).

For all these reasons, many constructors (myself included) now prefer making wide-open themeless crosswords over themed puzzles.

Another avenue being explored by the theme weary is special-category crosswords, a field that's taken off in the past ten years or so with the rise of the Internet. When I began writing golf-themed crosswords for the PGA Tour's Web site in 2000, fresh themes poured out: famous golf courses, players who've beaten Tiger Woods in head-to-head competition, and so forth. These themes would've been far too obscure for a mainstream puzzle, but were right down the fairway for the country club crowd. An added benefit of embracing a new category is the sudden spice in a previously well-traveled realm, three-, four-, and five-letter words. ISAO AOKI, a not-super-famous Japanese golfer whose first and last names are often called upon by desperate crosswords writers, suddenly ceased to be the semi-lousy entry he was in mainstream puzzles. And golf surnames like TWAY and OZAKI are short words that fit golf-loving solvers to—well, to a tee.

But this is a temporary fix; after about a hundred puzzles, "Golfer Ernie" or "Two-time U.S. Open Winner" for ELS had been used repeatedly, and the entry began to become stale in its own right.

Another ploy editors are taking to enliven themes is becoming more liberal in what kind of grid tricks they will allow. A recent *New York Sun* puzzle by Paula Gamache contained the theme entries BREAKTHROUGH, CROSS THE LINE, and the 18-letter THINK OUTSIDE THE BOX, which the attentive reader will notice does not fit in a 15 x 15 grid. For the word BOX, the solver had to draw a black box into an extra white square that protruded outside the bottom of the grid to accommodate the overlong phrase. A worthy gimmick, and the kind of clever rule breaking that editors are increasingly happy to partake in if it means a fresh theme.

Only time will tell what clever remedies constructors will come up with to breathe new life into the somewhat stagnant pool of crossword themes. The only guarantee is that they will try; whether they will succeed is anyone's guess.

• • •

"Macho" isn't a word that comes to mind when you think of crossword constructors; but I tell you that some of them are.

Pre-Shortz, the records for fewest number of words in a *New York Times*-published crossword was fifty-six, held by two constructors, Nancy Nicholson Joline and Kevin Boyle. Both record-setting grids contained some clunker entries, but that's unavoidable in such an extraordinarily wide open grid (the lower the word count, the more wide open the grid must be), and their fifty-six-word feats are made all the more impressive by having been achieved by Joline and Boyle in the pre-computerized gridmaking era.

The record was destined to fall once the machines took over, since weaving large fields of white is what the silicon monsters do best. When the computerized Frank Longo burst on the scene with a fifty-four-worder in 1997, he was hailed as the new record holder. One problem: it contained forty black squares, two more than the generally agreed-upon thirty-eight black square limit for a record holder (the more black squares you add to a grid the easier it is to fill, hence the need for an upper limit).

Longo answered critics in 2001 with another fifty-four worder containing only thirty-six black squares. It seemed like a record that might never be beaten, so he put the low-word count challenge aside for a while.

Then he heard that another constructor had started submit-ting fifty-four worders to Will Shortz, and Longo decided to go for the Holy Grail: he attempted to write a fifty-two-word puzzle. Opinions were divided on whether it was even pos-sible, but Longo managed to accomplish the task, strategically using common letter-rich phrases like DINETTE SETS and REMOTE SENSORS. Even with his talent and powerful database, the puzzle was hellishly difficult to write. "The bottom half of the grid was excruciating," he writes in a cruciverb.com piece on his feat, "and took at least two weeks."

Like toughs showing off their wheels, so a certain rarefied stratum of puzzle writer puffs his chest out by attempting a quantifiable feat of crossword constructing. Who can stack three sets of three fifteens in a grid, one on top of the other? Who can write a 15 x 15 with the lowest black square count? Who can beat Frank's fifty-two worder? These are questions the macho gridmasters ask themselves—and devote loads of time to when they decide to take a particular task on.

The lowest black square count record in a *Times* puzzle used to be twenty-one, held my Manny Nosowsky. When Joe DiPietro broke the record in 2001 with a lovely twenty-black-square grid, Nosowsky countered a few years later with a nineteen, a number which has yet to be bested. Low word count and low black square count records appear to be nearing their natural limit; each reduction in number of words or black squares is exponentially more difficult to achieve than the last, and even with increases in computer power, there are still only so many usable words and phrases in the language.

But keep an eye out for record-breaking achievements; there is ego on the line, and chest puffing, and some powerful computers out there with extremely bright people manipulating them. According to Longo's piece, Merl Reagle showed him a theoretically fillable grid with a word count of only fifty. Longo claims to have no intention of trying it, but time—and potential rivals—may change his mind.

Try this: a seven-letter word, begins and ends with an A, the clue is "Neighbor of Georgia."

Did you guess ALABAMA? Good, because that was the trap; the right answer is actually ARMENIA.

Not many solvers know this, but constructors set answer-specific traps like this all the time. It's not a coincidence that Armenia and Alabama both have seven letters, and that they have a couple of letters in common, and that he picked "Georgia" instead of "Azerbaijan." That constructor knew very well that you were going to put ALABAMA in there, and that's what he wanted you to do. If that seems mean, well, it is.

But it's also child's play. Try this one: five letters long, clue is "First letter in Greece."

Did you write ALPHA? If you did, I have the sad duty of informing you that you weren't even in the ballpark. ALPHA's the first trap answer in that clue; but a serious solver might have said "ALPHA would be too easy, let me take a second look," and come up with GAMMA, since the G in the Greek alphabet is that letter—hence it might be construed by a suitably twisted mind as the first letter in "Greece."

So if you came up with GAMMA—congratulations, you fell into the second trap the constructor set with that clue. If you didn't fall for ALPHA, he wanted you to fall for GAMMA. In fact he'd prefer that you fell for GAMMA, because then you thought you were outsmarting him, when he was actually outsmarting you.

The right answer is HARD G. I know, it's practically obnoxious—but that's crossword clues for you.

More so than the entries in the grid or even the theme, a crossword puzzle's clues determine its level of difficulty. TWO OF A KIND is a breeze when clued as "Identical twins, e.g.," but tough to get as "They were made for each other."

And the tricks they've got up their sleeves, these constructors; it's almost like they sit around all day trying to figure out ways to fool people. A five-letter word for "Petty matter?" ALBUM. A six-letter word for "Bologna sandwiches?" PANINI. An five-letter word for "Mark in the Water"? SPITZ.

That's the "masked capital letter" in action, one of the most underhanded clue tricks constructors have in their arsenal: we're talking about Tom Petty, the Italian city of Bologna, and olympic swimmer Mark Spitz. The constructor—an amoral creature on his best days—will not hesitate to exploit the convention of capitalizing the first word in each clue whether it needs it or not. Behind this capital letter may lurk much wickedness.

Sometimes the clue tricks are so devious they're borderline unfair, like "Italian flower" for ARNO. The Arno's a river, you're thinking, not a flower. Right, but "flower" here means "something that flows," so ARNO works.

But that's a little over the top—who really uses "flower" in that way?—so the polite thing to do in such cases is append a question mark to the end of the clue, which tips the solver off that some crazy wordplay hides in the mix. A thoughtful gesture, but sometimes a little like being told an asteroid's going to destroy the Earth in twenty-four hours: even forewarned, there's still not much you can do. The "?" at the end of "Go home?" doesn't help you much in getting JAPAN, after all (that's a recent mind-masher from ace constructor Brendan Emmett Quigley).

The first crossword ever published (in 1913; see next chapter) used mostly strict dictionary definitions as clues, such as "To cultivate." for FARM and "The plural of is." for ARE (each clue finished WASPishly with a period, too, a charming convention no longer in use today).

In the ninety-odd years since that first crossword, acceptable cluing methods have expanded from simple definitions only to include trivia ("1952 Olympics city" for OSLO), fill-in-the-blanks ("___ I help you?" for CAN), series of examples ("Apple, cherry, and lemon" for TREES), descriptive phrases ("Cuddly Chinese" for PANDA), and many other ways to point a solver toward the right answer.

Fill-in-the-blank clues are usually among the easiest in a puzzle, and experts know to attack those clues first when sitting down to solve. But even here danger may lurk, as those amoral constructors will use an apparently easy fill-in-the-blank to let you drop your guard. Peter Gordon once sprang "New York's Carnegie ___" on solvers for a four-letter word, knowing full well the majority would write in HALL, even though the answer was DELI.

A few constructors have even developed their own clue styles, such as Fred Piscop's "I Dare You" clues, which lard harmless words with sexual innuendo. Piscop has clued, for example, BUTTER as "Pat on the buns" or RETREAD as "Used Rubber." The clever calculus at play is that the same people who would be offended are precisely the same people who won't notice in the first place.

The advantage of regularly cluing tricky is like bluffing a lot in poker: people never know when you're being straight with them. Regular solvers of the *New York Times* puzzle are so used to Shortz's tricky clues that even a simple, vanilla clue like "Garfield, for example" for CAT would leave many hesitant to fill the answer in, so certain are they that there must be some kind of deviousness lurking.

I close the subject with a bizarre example from Peter Gordon in a recent *New York Sun* puzzle. To clue FIONA APPLE at 17-across, Gordon referenced the entire 90-word title of Apple's 1999 album, "When the Pawn Hits the Conflicts He Thinks Like a King What He Knows Throws the Blows When He Goes To the Fight and He'll Win the Whole Thing, 'Fore He Enters the Ring There's No Body To Batter When Your Mind Is Your Might So When You Go Solo, You Hold Your Own Hand and Remember That Depth Is the Greatest of Heights and If You Know Where You Stand, Then You Know Where to Land and If You Fall It Won't Matter, Cuz You'll Know That You're Right." To know that he was right about the title, Gordon actually purchased the album; in order to make the puzzle fit on one page, the rest of the clues tended toward being shorter than usual.

A fitting example with which to close a survey of the three parts of a crossword puzzle, for it illustrates that, as with themes and grids, constructors and editors continue to pump new oxygen into each part of their craft. Challenges await, of course, but life would be dull if they didn't.

CHAPTER 9

Orts

You don't see ORT much in crosswords anymore, and thank God for that. It's an obscure word meaning "table scrap" or "leftover piece of food," and used to be a standard in puzzles, along with ANOA and ESNE and the rest of the crosswordese gang.

I've never used it in a puzzle, but I'm calling it into service for this chapter's title. There are three areas of crosswords that didn't fit snugly elsewhere in this narrative, but they're orts worthy of human consumption: the early history of crosswords, British-style (cryptic) crosswords, and mistakes in crosswords. None is a full meal by itself, but I think the reader will appreciate the flavor.

The first crossword puzzle appeared in the *New York World* on December 21, 1913. Its creator was Arthur Wynne, a native of Liverpool who created a diamond-shaped grid with clues to fill an empty space in the "Fun" section of the paper that week. Wynne named the puzzle "Word-Cross," but a printing mistake three weeks later changed the name accidentally to "Cross Word," which stuck.

In the mid-1920s crosswords briefly became a craze, due in large part to the publication of the first crossword puzzle book in 1924. People who had never done one in their entire lives suddenly flocked to crossword puzzle–solving contests; according to puzzle author Coral Amende, "Due to greatly increased demand, the New York Public Library was forced to limit users' dictionary time to five minutes each." Tunesmiths even cranked out popular songs about the new mania, with titles like "Since Ma's Gone Crazy over Cross Word Puzzles" and "Crossword Mamma, You Puzzle Me (But Papa's Gonna Figure You Out)."

This boom subsided, as booms must, but crosswords were no passing fad. Over time they became a newspaper staple, and every major paper in the Unites States has one today (the last holdout, the *Wall Street Journal*, caved in 1998).

The crossword puzzle has ancient antecedents. So-called "word squares" were used by the Romans, simple square patterns where the same word read across and down, as in this famous example:

SATOR

AREPO

TENET

OPERA

ROTAS

An especially elegant piece of work, since its words are reversals of each other (the central word TENET being a palindrome), and the five words taken together spell a sentence (translations vary, but it's something like "the farmer Arepo holds the wheels with effort").

It does show that people had been thinking about and using crossword-esque forms long before Wynne showed up on the scene. Amusingly, it may also be the first example of crosswordese, since the name AREPO is suspiciously unusual, according to scholars, and was possibly created by the word square's unknown author to complete his puzzle. It's charming to think that a wordsmith 2,000-plus years ago hauled out a borderline entry just to make the words fit, precisely as crossword writers still do today.

Like Darwin cobbling together his theory of evolution from both original research and the work of others, the ideas behind the crossword had been experimented with in bits and pieces before, but Arthur Wynne was the first to put them all together in a form we would recognize today as a crossword puzzle. For this he gets his place in crossword history; that first puzzle even had an impish bit of wit in it, at the clue labeled "18-19," which read "What this puzzle is." and which yielded the answer HARD. Rather clever for the first go-round, and indicative of the sort of mind that makes these things in the first place.

If Lewis Carroll took mushrooms, then didn't sleep for three days straight, then drank a bottle of wine, and only then sat down to write a word puzzle, it might look like a cryptic crossword.

Cryptics, also called "British-style crosswords," are the slightly insane cousin of the American crossword. Why are they so odd? They don't generally have themes, but neither do lots of American puzzles, so no big difference there. Cryptic grids are merely skeletal, unlike the more filled-in American grids, but they're still recognizably crosswords. So again, some difference, but nothing too major.

The key to cryptics is the clues: while Brits can quickly grasp the straightforward cluing styles of American puzzles—"Turquoise cousin" for TEAL or "Lunch order, for short" for BLT, say—cryptic crossword clues are so nutty looking that your first thought might be to wonder if there's been a printing error.

"Photographers heckle this writer following Hemingway (9)," reads 15-across in a recent cryptic by Canadian puzzle writer Fraser Simpson. The answer is PAPARAZZI. "Foolishly rent Tampa's penthouses, for example (10)," reads 13-down. The answer is APARTMENTS.

Weird, eh? Instead of a normal definition, or some other straightforward hint at the answer as in an American puzzle, cryptics take the Rube Goldberg path, employing all kinds of wordplay en route: anagrams, reversals, words hidden inside other words, and so on. Every cryptic clue contains an American-style definition of its answer word somewhere in it, but also a form of wordplay leading in a second path to that same answer, and often an indicator as to what sort of wordplay is being employed. The length of answer words is also given in parentheses at the end of the clue so the solver will know if the answer is multiword; an eight-letter clue with the answer GLASS JAW would have (5,3) appended to it.

Sound forbidding? Let's take a look: in the PAPARAZZI clue above, we find the American-style definition of the answer in the word "Photographers." Then we have a charades-like series of word parts leading to that same answer as well: "heckle" is RAZZ, "this writer" is I, and they both come after ("following") PAPA, which was Hemingway's nickname. PAPA+RAZZ+I. What could be simpler?

For the second clue, we have an anagram lurking. "penthouses, for example" is the American-style definition pointing to APARTMENTS, while "rent Tampa's" anagrams into that same answer, and "Foolishly" is an indicator that an anagram is in order. That may seem like a stretch, but any word indicating carelessness or disorder can hint that letters need to be rearranged.

And the clues get much wackier from there. Almost any kind of wordplay is fair game, as long as it's fairly hinted at in the clue. A 1992 Henry Hook cryptic featured this for an eight-letter answer: "Debut of 'Top Gun' primarily shown in moviehouses." The answer was THEATERS: "Debut of 'Top" is T—because that is the first letter, or "debut" of the word "top"—HEATER is old slang for "Gun," and "Primarily shown" is S—the "primary" letter of the word "shown," you might say, is an S. Which leaves "moviehouses," or THE-ATERS. The "in" before "moviehouses" in the clue is the kind of little word that's sometimes added for sentence flow to a cryptic, but plays no part in the answer.

Another cute example is the title of a 2003 book on cryptic crosswords written by Anglo-South African journalist Sandy Balfour. *Pretty Girl in Crimson Rose (8)* is the title, and also a cryptic clue yielding the word REBELLED, as follows: "Crimson" is RED, while "Pretty Girl" is BELLE; put the "pretty girl in crimson," or place the word BELLE within RED, and you get REBELLED, which is defined by the last word in the clue, "Rose."

Cryptics have generally appeared in American magazines that want to seem a cut above the newspapers and magazines that carry standard crosswords: the *Nation, Harper's,* the *New Yorker,* and the *Atlantic Monthly* are all magazines that carry or have carried in the past a cryptic (the *Atlantic* recently moved its long-running cryptic by Emily Cox and Henry Rathvon from the print magazine to the Web site only, which elicited howls of protest from the crossword community).

There is indeed something precious and a bit pretentious about cryptics, but they're really not that hard to get a handle on, after a little practice. Still, they are an acquired taste more likely to stay popular on their home side of the Atlantic, where their place in the native culture is already well established. Sudoku's recent rise has probably sucked all the oxygen out of the public's desire for new puzzle types anyway, at least for a while.

Mistakes happen in crosswords. Not that often, but inevitably, even in the most scrutinized, power-edited puzzles around. No matter how many editors, proofreaders, fact-checkers, and testers a puzzle has, those thousands or millions of solvers in the general population are eventually going to call the editor out on something or other that's slipped through the cracks.

That's not a bad thing in and of itself, but the sheer joy solvers take in finding mistakes can be off-putting. In a puzzle for Major League Baseball's Web site, I once erroneously referred to Dodger third baseman Ron Cey as a catcher. I received a nasty e-mail from a solver pointing out my mistake, and it ended with a gratuitous "So, what's your problem?"

This is typical of the haughty tone mistake-nabbing solvers take. I think it's a kind of revenge: they've been zapped so many times by the puzzlemakers in the past that they want to twist the knife a little when the situation's finally reversed.

Will Shortz says that about twenty errors get past him every year at the *Times*. That's from over 30,000 clues, so quite a batting average, and more impressive when you realize that Shortz doesn't shy away from using new, intriguing clues as often as he does. If an editor's goal is limited to having zero errors in the puzzle, it's easily attainable by simply using dull, no-risk clues. MILAN clued as "Italian city" will never be wrong, but will never be exciting, either; MILAN clued as "City founded by the Celts around 600 B.C." or "Location of Giorgio Armani's headquarters" is much more lively, but the added facts give errors a chance to creep in.

Many things can cause an error to appear in a crossword: a gap in the knowledge of the editor or test solver; simple human oversight; and, sometimes, the editor's reference book itself being wrong. When I visited Will Shortz at his home, he showed me the reference book he relied on to ascertain for a clue that Canada's Fundy National Park is in Nova Scotia, when it's actually in New Brunswick. Canadian readers called him out on it, but what can the guy do when his reference book has the facts wrong?

What's far more common than an error finding its way into a crossword is for a solver to mistakenly think they've found an error in a puzzle and write the editor about it. Shortz once received an angry letter from a solver who was unable to find in any of her reference books the word GOUP, which Shortz had clued in a puzzle as "Rise." She was indignant, sneering: "I don't know what dictionary *you're* using." I wonder if she ever figured it out.

Echoing Shortz's experience, I had an e-mail in 2004 from a Jonesin' solver who couldn't understand the word DOUP clued as "Fix, as a hairstyle." He provided online references showing that DOUP was only some Scottish dialect word meaning "the buttocks," and chided me for allowing such an obscure entry in the puzzle.

The general rule crossword editors follow is "look anything up you're not sure of," but this leads to problems, since it doesn't address the true source of errors. The thought process that most gets editors in trouble is not laziness in failing to look up references they're not sure of; it's being "sure" about an answer and therefore failing to look it up, then finding out later the thing they were sure of was wrong.

For instance, I had a puzzle once submitted to me that had clued ELO as " 'Hold the Line' group." I know the band and the song well, so there was no need to look this answer up—except that it's wrong. "Hold the Line" was a song by Toto, another band I know well. Why the mistake then?

ELO has two famous songs called "Hold on Tight" and "Telephone Line," and those crossed in my head when the puzzle writer suggested in his clue that "Hold the Line" was ELO. It's not the stuff you don't know that gets you; it's the stuff you're 100 percent certain of.

This has led one editor to suggest that *everything* be looked up, which is silly; but when on heightened alert in the days after an error has slipped by on my watch, I do find myself questioning even the simplest of clues. "Cat's sound" for MEOW? Cats do meow, right? Or is it dogs? Let me Google that . . .

CHAPTER 10

Henry Hook

"Henry probably won't talk to you," a former colleague of his at *GAMES* tells me at Stamford. "You should think about interviewing someone else, like Merl."

"Well, Merl's great—but I really would like to talk to Henry."

The ex-colleague grimaces in understanding. "Well, you can try. Do you know about Henry's—"

I interrupt with a nod, and he nods back. Then a short silence, a bit of respect for the subject of death.

"Henry's had some bad things happen to him in his life," he finally intones, carefully. And after another moment:

"Henry's a misanthrope."

Henry Hook wrote a crossword that mesmerized me when I was a teenager. Along the bottom right corner he'd stacked the entries AZERBAIJAN, SOMETIMES Y ("End of a schoolroom mnemonic"), and LUXURY TAX. All those expensive letters and quirky words jumping around each other with exquisite choreography; it was art. I never understood paintings or sculpture or even music, but this I appreciated, and this Henry Hook was the artist I most admired.

Henry Hook is the third greatest American crossword puzzle constructor of all time, according to an informal poll I conduct among constructors and solvers at cruciverb.com. He gets my vote, but the crowd picks Merl Reagle for the top spot, and Manny Nosowsky for second.

One of the Reagle voters—a former ACPT champion—explains his choice: "Henry was second, and in another moment might have been first." He means that Hook has grown weary of standard crosswords in the past decade or so, and focused more on cryptics, acrostics, and other variety puzzles, so the crosswords-only specialist Reagle got his nod.

Another solver writes: "My vote goes to Henry Hook as the most diabolical constructor I've ever faced. Henry Hook—master of the bastard!"

I've been told to call Wayne Schmittberger, longtime editor in chief of *GAMES Magazine,* to ask advice about getting Henry to talk to me. I'd been informed that he knows Hook well, but Schmittberger just sighs into the phone when I tell him what I'm after.

"I mean, I haven't talked to Henry in years," he pleads. "I think I have an e-mail address someplace, but I don't know if it's current." In fact, no one in crosswords has seen Henry for six years, since he last showed up at Stamford. He is famously reclusive.

Schmittberger eventually digs it up and gives it to me,

then adds, "I don't think this address is going to work, but if it does, don't tell him I gave it to you."

I met Henry Hook once, for about 45 seconds, at Stamford in 1997. Round 5 had just ended, and the puzzle's author, Mike Shenk, was standing outside the main ballroom talking with Hook. It happened to be St. Patrick's Day, and the theme of Shenk's puzzle had been phrases with the letters ST. PAT ensconced in them: TEST PATTERNS, LOST PATIENCE, the New Jersey city of EAST PATERSON, and so on.

I approached them and addressed Shenk: "Hi Mike, I wanted to tell you that I think your Round 5 puzzle was just pathetic."

Both Shenk and Hook stared in disbelief at my overt rudeness.

Then I added, "Get it? JUST PATHETIC?"

They both had the "a-ha" moment; Shenk grinned, but Hook grabbed my shoulder and made a mock motion like he was going to knock me out.

I introduced myself and we shook hands, but I was so starstruck that I walked off without saying anything further. I only remember thinking how cool it was that Henry Hook had just joked around with me, pretending to punch my lights out.

When Hook doesn't e-mail me back, I figure the address wasn't good, or maybe he just doesn't want to talk. I consider interviewing Merl Reagle instead, or maybe someone else, but it doesn't seem right. Plucking up my nerve, I switch-board.com his number in Brooklyn and call it.

"That was you?" Hook exclaims. "I thought it was spam. If I don't recognize an e-mail address I just delete it, with these viruses going around. Have you heard about this latest one?"

When I say I'd like to interview him, he's suspicious at first. "Why would you wanna talk to *me*?" and then "What's this book about exactly?" After some imploring and cajoling and flattery, he finally gives a little ground: "If you want you can come up and we'll talk, but I doubt you'll find anything to write about."

Henry Hook surveys the menu and finds something he doesn't like. "I hate how they say 'two eggs, any style,'" he gripes, his finger pressed firmly against the offending brunch selection. "It's like, alright, I'll take mine Dutch Colonial.'"

I laugh out loud—his delivery and what're-ya-gonna-do? hand gestures are terrific—but Hook gives me a dismissive wave in response. "Ah, that's not funny. Get over it. But really, I just can't consider 'scrambled' a 'style.'"

Henry Hook has lost a lot of people. His father drove a delivery truck for a liquor store in East Rutherford, New Jersey, where Henry was raised. "He was gone every morning before I got up for school, and he wouldn't come home until ten or eleven o'clock at night." He worked Saturdays, too. "My image of my father is him sitting passed out in his easy chair on Sunday afternoons in front of a ball game."

He died of leukemia when Henry was seventeen. "He wasn't even sick," Hook says, "and three weeks later he was gone."

• • •

For Henry Hook, these are lean times. He writes the Sunday crossword every other week for the *Boston Globe Magazine*, plus a daily mini-puzzle for a syndicate. But he recently lost his third source of income, doing two puzzle books a year for Random House, when the publisher cut back on its catalog. His older books are mostly out of print now, and only the occasional, tiny royalty check trickles in from them.

"Unless something comes up, this is gonna be a tough year," Hook says. He can fill the gap partially with free-lancing, but that doesn't pay very well. "I've put out feelers; everyone knows I need work, but nobody's calling me."

His expenses keep rising as neighborhood rents go up and advancing age requires further medical attention, so it's a bad time for his income to go down. "I've always had a roof over my head, but I'll never be able to retire. I'd like to but the New York State Lottery Commission won't let me. I keep telling them what numbers to pull but I get no cooperation from them whatsoever."

Henry Hook is fifty years old, tallish, heavyset, with a round baby face and bright eyes that seem brightest right as he's delivering a wry, W. C. Fields–style punch line. The weight situation has been improving since he found out last year that he's diabetic; since then he's been consuming more vegetables, fewer carbs, and virtually no alcohol, though he was never much more than a casual Bud Light drinker anyway. I think he's bald, but he never removes his black baseball cap during the six hours we spend at his Park Slope hangout, a Cajun-Italian joint with a bar called Two Boots, so I can't be sure.

He'd mentioned Scrabble during our meal, and that he plays a woman named Kristy here at the restaurant several nights a week, so I challenge him to a game and he accepts. Normally I'd feel self-conscious taking up a restaurant table with a board game, but the staff here knows Hook and they're fine with it. When he starts to get up from the table to retrieve the board, our young waitress waves him off: "No Henry, let me get that for you."

"A few of these tiles have been altered, but it's a complete set," Hook informs me, holding out for my perusal a V that has been extended via magic marker to a Y. It's more than just a few tiles: my first rack includes both an I that someone changed into a K and an N that has awkwardly morphed into M (later we'll lose a real M under the table, and I'll have to take a black pen to a spare N myself to replace it).

These makeshift alterations make anagramming a little dodgy, so I start with CONK for 20 points, mostly to get the particularly distracting K-that-was-an-I off my rack.

Playing immediately, Hook hooks KIWI down off my K for nineteen. "I am officially one point behind you," he proclaims. Hook plays eight to ten games per week, always at this restaurant, always with Kristy.

"Are you two . . . ?" I ask.

"Are we what?" Hook snaps.

"You know, together?"

He shakes his head. "She's married. We're just friends."

I play a 26-pointer, which Hook counters with the pretty bingo RETYPES/CONKS for 85.

Suddenly a woman's voice pipes up: "I knew you were cheating on me!" It's Kristy, who's just wandered in from the bar, where she's been playing Boggle.

"It was his idea," Hook pleads.

Kristy is a thin, fortyish woman with glasses, curly dark hair, and a face with Greek features. "Well, I'm just glad you've found a worthy opponent," she says, then adds to me in a stage whisper: "I've only beaten him once in about a year of trying. I have the score sheet on my refrigerator."

She disappears back into the bar area and Hook goes on a tear, bingoing with FADEOUTS for 74, and then ORDERING for 66. The final score is a slaughter: 451-286.

"Ouch," I say.

He looks pleased and lets me know it: "That wasn't just a win, that was a humiliation."

On the train ride to meet him, I'd made a quick list of my five favorite Henry Hook crosswords, all five from years ago. Later, I ask him which of all his puzzles is his personal favorite.

"If I knew which puzzle caused the most solvers the most grief, that would be the one," he replies. I press, but he won't give me a real answer. When I mention two of my favorites to him, he claims to not remember either one. "Come on, I don't believe you," I chide. "How can you not remember these two?"

"Look," he explodes, "I've written thousands of crosswords. Thousands. This is just work for me. I don't enjoy it. Work: see 'drudgery.' "

• • •

I want revenge, so we follow the first game of Scrabble with a second. "You must be a glutton for punishment," he brags, but I draw an A and warn, "this looks like it's going to be my game," since unless Hook draws a blank or an A, I'll be going first. He draws an S, so I get to start. This is Henry Hook, but I don't care: I'm still pissed he crushed me the first game and plan on returning the compliment.

My opening rack is EIMNOTW, but the W is an altered V and I've got the M-that-used-to-be-an-N again, so the word-forming confusion returns. I finally play WOMEN; I don't know if it was the best move, but I had to get that W and M off my rack.

We trade medium-scoring shots for a while until I bingo with VALISES and take a 76-point lead. Hook turns pessimistic and serious: "Looks like this really is going to be your game." But he hangs tough and eventually comes back to eke out a 316-297 win. It stings a little, especially since I had what I thought was a sure bingo ensemble late in the game, but couldn't convert: DEGINT and a blank tile was the rack, and I had an H and a T to play off of.

The next day I'll receive an e-mail from Hook: "i checked—you didn't have any bingos."

Henry Hook had one sibling, an older brother named Grant. With an eleven-year age difference and some bad blood between them, the Hook brothers were never close; the last time they saw each other was in 1986, when they cleaned out their just-deceased mother's apartment. The last time they had any contact at all was a few months later, when Grant declined an invitation to Henry's wedding.

Last year, a cousin called to inform Hook that his brother had died.

"Did you go to his funeral?"

Hook shakes his head. "I don't even know if he had one."

No one who knew him thought Henry Hook would ever find someone to love. He was too bristly, too negative, too sarcastic. Lifelong bachelorhood looked like the most probable course ahead. But then he met Stephanie Abrams at a small gathering of puzzlers in Boston in 1985, and they were married the following year. Hook moved up to live with her.

"She told me early on, when it looked like we were going to be more than friends, that she had cystic fibrosis. And she said, look, if you want to run, I'll understand. But by that time I was already in love with her."

She began publishing crosswords under the byline Stephanie Abrams-Hook. The pair spent a lot of time together at home, enjoying each other's companionship, companionship of a depth that Henry had not experienced before. "It was the only happy time in my life," he says. They were married for four years, and then she died.

"She was the highlight of my life," Hook says.

Henry Hook has a bad knee and can't afford health insurance. Last year during a hospital visit, Hook was informed that the knee might require surgery. He began crying and had a minor breakdown in the emergency room, and the doctors assigned him a social worker, whom he still sees regularly.

It was the despair of his situation that seemed to dawn on him in that episode: fifty years old, no close family left; no close friends; dwindling professional ties and contacts; the eternal bitter sting that Stephanie had been taken away from him. And now, medical bills and surgery he couldn't pay for. And even if he could, no one to take care of him during a recovery period.

"I've always had a loathing for the human race," he tells me, in another context.

Merl Reagle self-syndicated his crossword puzzles beginning in the 1970s, and has done well for himself. Will Shortz, through both skill and charisma, has jumped from one prestige post in puzzles to the next. I hustled for magazine and Web site and newspaper customers and have done OK as well.

But Henry hasn't done any of these things, and this is why he struggles financially. He wants his puzzles to speak for themselves, but in puzzles, as in other fields, contacts matter. That people know and like you matters. But Henry "barely tolerates other human beings," as Kristy puts it, and this has led him to be less well-off moneywise than he deserves to be.

It isn't fair, what is, though?

Enough Scrabble. We move over to the bar area, where Kristy's knocking back glasses of white wine the goateed bartender keeps pouring her, even after she's paid her tab. Like Henry, she's a regular.

Kristy's brother, it turns out, is Todd Wilkerson, the actor who plays the king in recent Burger King commercials. "He wears a mask," Kristy says, "and it's really heavy. But my brother never complains, and there aren't many six-foot-five actors willing to wear that heavy mask and never complain about it."

Henry describes Kristy as "my best friend these days," though she'll later tell me she's never been to his nearby house. I ask what she does, and between sips she says, "I'm an executive assistant. You know, a secretary." I see why Hook likes Kristy: she's positive, smiles and laughs a lot, and likes to spend time with Henry, but she's also married and therefore inaccessible. Given Hook's losses in life, this must be part of the attraction.

The subject of conversation moves to her single victory over her teacher.

"I e-mailed my husband that I'd beaten Henry in Scrabble, and he writes back, in all capital letters, 'OH MY GOD!' "

"I felt so good. I was like, 'I'm broke, I have no food in my house, but look, I beat Henry in Scrabble.' I should laminate that scoresheet."

A few months ago, Will Shortz used a puzzle Henry sent him on his weekly NPR *Puzzlemaster* segment. Hook gives the puzzle to me: name an eight-letter noun that has a B in it somewhere, in which you pluralize the noun by putting an S *before* the B. Good puzzle, I see why Shortz used it; it takes me about a minute to get: PASSERBY.

Kristy regales me with the story: "Everyone in this whole bar was like, 'Oh my God, they mentioned Henry's name on NPR and they had one of his puzzles on the air!' "

"It was not a big deal," Henry scoffs, but I can tell he likes the attention. "I'm in a business where I stumble upon quirks in the language, and that was a quirk in the language."

The bartender says "hold on a second" and returns a minute later with a copy of a crossword Henry made for the bar's Mardi Gras party last month. It's a skeletal grid, but every word in it uses only the letters in MARDI GRAS. 24-down is DISARM ("Win over" is the clue); 18-down is DAIS ("Setting for roasts and toasts"); 22-across is DIAGRAM ("You're filling it in").

Later, after I've had a couple of Rolling Rocks, I'll say to Kristy: "Do you people in the bar know who this guy is? I mean, do you know that he's the best at what he does?"

Kristy laughs and shrugs her shoulders. "I don't know, he's just Henry," she giggles. "Come to think of it, I don't know who the fuck he is!"

When I ask what kind of kid he was, Hook fires the answer back right away: "A loner. A bookworm. Antisocial. I mean, I was a good student. The teachers liked me." He watched a lot of TV—cartoons and game shows mostly, like *Concentration* and the Art Fleming *Jeopardy!*

"I loved the old *Jeopardy!* because it wasn't automated. There were actually two guys back there yanking the cards out, and every once in a while one of them would get stuck and Art would have to ad-lib."

After his father passed away, Hook went to work in a drugstore to help support his mother. He also enrolled at William Paterson College (now William Paterson University), where he majored in mathematics. "It's a useless degree," Hook says. "I don't think I'd make a good math teacher."

It was during college that Hook had his first crossword published—in the *New York Times*, at age nineteen. "During the Will Weng Administration," he jokes. "When writing puzzles was something I did after work, for fun, I felt better about it. But my stuff's not as good now as it used to be. I consider that I'm a little over the hill."

When I tell Hook that people still appreciate his work, he responds: "Yeah, I know, but I can't control that."

Hook puts away Diet Coke after Diet Coke, I'm on my fourth Rolling Rock, and Kristy is playing with her fourth glass of wine (that I've seen).

"Why don't you hang out with crossword people?" I ask Henry. It just seems such a waste for him to spend so much time alone when there's this community of people nearby whose world he's a superstar in.

"They're boring," Hook says, which I don't understand. Even if he does find puzzlers a little dull, not to lay eyes on a single one in six years seems excessive; there's something more going on beneath the surface, but I don't know what.

I press Hook for one person in puzzles whom he likes, whose company he has enjoyed at some point in the past thirty-plus years. After insisting there isn't anyone, he finally relents: "I guess I would say Mike Shenk." Their desks were next to each other at *GAMES*, "and we'd banter back and forth, finish each other's jokes, stuff like that." But he hasn't seen or even e-mailed Shenk in six years, since he'd last been at Stamford. Someone from

Shenk's puzzle-writing company did contact Henry a few years ago to do some rebuses for Snapple, who wanted to use them on the underside of their bottlecaps for a contest. But he doesn't recall having any contact with Shenk himself.

I ask him, off the record, if he has any enemies in crosswords. "The solvers, mostly," he quips, with Hollywood timing and delivery. It could have been said by Groucho Marx himself.

After writing crosswords for a living for so many years, Hook is restless and burnt out. When I ask what his ideal project would be at this point in his career, he says, "I would do a book of all kinds of puzzles except straight crosswords. There's gotta be something else besides crosswords or it's gonna make me crazy."

This ennui actually makes Hook's crosswords more intriguing, since you can see—have been able to see for years, in fact—that he pushes himself with bizarre twists to include something unique in each puzzle. Sometimes this will mean a gratuitous number in a grid where a letter should be, or a puzzle that's actually a pirate's treasure map—or occasionally, something mischievous. Hook once did a puzzle for a magazine noted for prudishness in terms of what content they allow in their puzzles—nothing the slightest bit risqué, ever. The answer to 1-across he made FUCHSIA, and the clue something vague that didn't even suggest the answer was a color, or a plant.

Then he made the clues for 1-, 2-, and 3-down very easy, so the solver would get those three answers first, and their hearts would race as they imagined what on earth 1-across could possibly be.

After Stephanie died, Hook moved back to Brooklyn from Boston. "I've lived in New Jersey, Boston, and Brooklyn," he says. "Someday I hope to live in a place where people pronounce the letter R."

Hook lives alone in a one-level house in Park Slope that he's rented since 1993. Before that he lived across the street, "but that landlord was an asshole," so he moved thirty feet across the asphalt (his street number went from 20 to 21). "There are boxes everywhere since I thought I'd have to move, but now I might not have to."

He likes working at home; it suits his personality: "I don't have to face co-workers, and it's always casual Friday." He usually wakes up early and works all morning. "I like to be done by noon," he claims, after which he usually heads over to Two Boots. He used to stay at home and do nothing in the afternoons and evenings until the smoking ban in New York City took effect a couple of years ago. "I used to go to the Carriage House, but there'd be one person smoking across the room and I'd go home and be coughing all night. The cigarette ban gave me a social life."

There's something in this whole conversation I just don't buy, something incongruous. Hook is supposed to be this misanthrope, this reclusive ogre, yet the person I've talked on the phone and e-mailed and spent the afternoon with is not like that at all: he is animated, socially adept, interesting, and constantly cracking jokes ("This place near my house had a sign up that said they sold 'Essential Oils.' I went over and looked and thought, 'nope, I don't need 'em!')".

He's got Kristy, me, and the bartender rolling in the aisles. A little curmudgeonly with the commentary, maybe, but it seems like even those comments are made out of habit; they don't really fit him anymore. People seem to like Henry, and he seems to like human attention and camaraderie.

I tell him all this, emboldened by the beer. I tell him that I don't understand why the lively person I've spent the last six hours with is such a hermit, why he shuts himself off from others still, so many years later.

He may be turning a corner in life, he lets on. He's begun dating again, for one—he posted an ad on craigslist and went out on a date a couple of weeks before. It didn't go great, but at least he's out there. "I think it's just growing older," he says. "I'm tired of being alone."

Kristy has gone home and the clock reads 8:20. I know that Henry is not a night owl and it's probably time to go.

"You got everything you need for this?" he asks.

"I think so."

We walk out into the Brooklyn Saturday night and I notice for the first time how pronounced his limp is; the knee must be really bad. "How far away's your house?" I ask.

"Not far if I take the bus." Walking even medium distances is difficult.

"Alright, Henry, this was great."

"Was my pleasure," he says, and walks across the street to his bus stop, as I continue on toward my train station.

I'm still buzzing from the beer, and I spend the eight-minute walk thinking how nice it would be for this person to have some joy in his sixth decade of life, some real joy again, and a warm feeling comes over me, since I am cautiously optimistic that it might actually happen.